LANDMARK COLLECTOR'S LIBRARY

THE SPIRIT OF HULLAND
THE 20TH CENTURY IN PHOTOGRAPHS

Hulland, Hulland Ward & Biggin-by-Hulland

David Phillipson

Published by

Landmark Publishing Ltd
Ashbourne Hall, Cokayne Ave, Ashbourne, Derbyshire DE6 1EJ England
Tel: (01335) 347349 Fax: (01335) 347303
e-mail: landmark@clara.net
web site: www.landmarkpublishing.co.uk

ISBN 1 84306 067 1

Print: Bookcraft, Midsomer Norton
Design: Mark Titterton
Cover: James Allsopp

Front cover: The Blacksmiths Cottage, 1911; **Back cover top:** Hulland Grange, c.1900; **Middle:** Ashbourne
Carnival 1981, Hulland Scouts; **Bottom:** Queen Elizabeth II opening Carsington Reservoir, 1992;
Title page: Ashbourne Carnival 1981, Hulland Cubs.

LANDMARK COLLECTOR'S LIBRARY

THE SPIRIT OF
HULLAND

THE 20TH CENTURY IN PHOTOGRAPHS

Hulland, Hulland Ward & Biggin-by-Hulland

David Phillipson

Landmark Publishing

CONTENTS

AUTHOR'S NOTE & ACKNOWLEDGEMENTS

No book such as this could be written without the help of a good many people, villagers and others. Some – and they know who they are – have contributed beyond the call of duty with both reminiscence and precious photographs, putting me in the way of other rewarding lines of enquiry and generally entering in to the spirit of the thing. My gratitude to them is great. So many folk have helped me – and I hope they will regard this as their book as much as mine – that I can only list them here in alphabetical order, regardless of individual contributions. I earnestly trust that I have included all my respondents in the list which follows and beg the forgiveness of anyone overlooked; so easily done among so many:

Linda and David Abrahart, Alf and Betsy Allsop, Pauline Birkett, Richard Blackwall, George Briddon, Mr A Childs, Mr & Mrs P Coleman, Maxwell Craven, Robert and Shirley Dale, Robert Day, Anne Deakin, Rosie Dias, D. Dorricott, Mr William Fearn, Ian Glover, Mr Phil Hall, Mrs Pat Holburn, Mr Charles Hooley, Edith and David Hough, Margaret Lake, Mr K McGhee, Margaret Milewski, Mrs D O'Gara, Richard Ormsby, Jean Redfern, Mr Frank Rodgers MBE, Ron Russell, Rex Sevier, Mr Mike Simmons, Mrs Lesley Slack, Chris and Lesley Taylor, Richard Thraves, Alice Warner, Roy Webster, Gordon Wheatcroft, Evelyn Willets, Daphne Wood.

My grateful thanks are due to Carol Evans of Severn Trent Press Office; also to Carol Seal of the *Derby Evening Telegraph* Photographic Department. I would like here to record my appreciation of that journal's accessibility to researchers of archive material.

Finally to Lindsey Porter and all the staff at Landmark Publishing who so civilly hid their dismay at hearing my tread on the stairs, again.

DJP
Millington Green

July 2002

This is the story, told in pictures, of an ordinary Derbyshire village, undistinguished enough to the casual traveller on his way to somewhere else; not on any tourist's itinerary except, perhaps, in recent years, those heading for the amenities of Carsington Water. Its most loyal son or daughter would not describe Hulland Ward as picturesque, though odd corners of its close neighbour and progenitor, Hulland village, deserve the epithet. Arthur Mee in his "Derbyshire", published in 1937, says of Hulland Ward: *At the end of a fine ridge of high land, it has a magnificent outlook over the hills and moors...* So it does, and there are few householders in Hulland Ward who do not enjoy a splendid view of rolling countryside from their windows.

The village has played its humble part down the years in great events, and made its sacrifices, as the war memorial in its churchyard – one of the many hundreds to be seen in villages throughout the kingdom – bears witness. It has seen a steady if unspectacular growth in population during the century recently ended, from 392 souls in 1900 to 1,030 today, with much of that increase housed on the "new" estate built in the mid-1960s.

Such changes as have taken place in Hulland Ward and its environs over a hundred years are but a microcosm of those in the nation at large; a little slower and gentler perhaps, in keeping with the pace of life in the countryside. Piped water arrived only in 1935, making Hulland's many common wells redundant, with mains sewerage not until 1950, and then only for the lucky villagers; dwellers beyond its boundaries made their own arrangements, and still do, by way of cesspits and septic tanks. Thus by mid-century Hulland Ward enjoyed all the blessings of modern civilization: mains water, gas, electricity, a village policeman and a railway station three miles down the road at Shottle; the last two having themselves become victims of "progress" in recent years.

At the beginning of this story, most inhabitants of Hulland Ward were farmers and farmworkers, with the usual leavening of rural craftsmen: blacksmiths, harness maker and wheelwright-carpenter doubling as village undertaker, whose employment was always secure. Today, few villagers still work on the land; most Hulland folk travel far and wide to their work in surrounding cities and towns. Despite that, or because of it, present-day Hulland Ward displays – to this writer at least, an "incomer" (or outsider!) a strong sense of community; a tone set by its older residents, a surprising number of whom in this age of increasing mobility are Hulland born and bred, who married locally and brought up their children here.

If one thing has become clear to this observer in the course of his researches, it is that "ordinary", despite its use in the foregoing, is not a word to describe Hulland Ward. If the trouble is taken to burrow a little beneath the surface, any centuries-old habitation will, it goes without saying, yield some rich veins of social history. In Hulland Ward and its close surroundings there are many, mostly but by no means exclusively among the elderly, with a deep consciousness of their community's past – and marked views about its present! It is they who have made this book.

Chapter 1 – Village & Villagers: Then and Now

That Hulland Ward, and neighbouring Hulland village, has changed relatively little in the course of a century is manifest in the pictures which follow; so many landmarks and buildings unaltered and readily recognisable today. There is an air of timelessness in the early images; scenes bathed in ancient sunlight, peopled with villagers young and old who no doubt would have been conscious, in a religious age, of their mortality: but aware or not, mostly returned to dust by now. Though if immortality is achieved through posterity, Hulland Ward is more fortunate than most, for many present-day villagers recognise their grand and great-grand-parents, aunts and uncles, in them.

How *quiet* it must have been then, living along that empty, dusty road – hard to imagine today. Birdsong, shouts of children, creak and swish of a passing bicycle, rattle of a cart... The first few motor-cars to pass through must have brought people rushing to their doors! Still, even today at certain times, one can drive the five miles to Ashbourne along an empty road – and there aren't too many parts of the country where that is possible as the 21st century dawns.

Above: John Beeston was one of the two village blacksmiths in 1911, the date of this photograph. His cottage, pictured, is the last building on the south side of the main road above the "Nag's Head" inn. It is called The Smithy now and is modernised, with rendering and larger windows.

View of "Bottom End" about 1908. The pond and site of the old outbuildings now lie under the "Black Horse" car park.

Ward Gate, 1902. "Boys and girls come out to play" – but strictly segregated, of course.

Above: A charming little group captured by the lens in 1910 and showing the tiny general store at the western end of Hulland Moss. Old Mr Cheadle, straw-hatted, holds the hand of his grandson Eric, beside whom stands little Evelyn Taylor, both resplendent in frilly Sunday-best. Eric's parents lean on the gate, while Mrs Milward, shopkeeper, stares mistrustfully at the camera from the shop door.

Surely the smallest dwelling in Hulland Ward. Wheel Cottage *(above)* in 1904, and *(left)* today. Unchanged externally except for the bricked-up window in the earlier photo, which seems to date the cottage pre-1782, when Window Tax was almost doubled.

Above: Another view of "Bottom End" Hulland Ward which shows clearly the divergence of highways eastwards from the village. Belper Road, Derby Road and Moss Lane off to the left.

Below: Christ Church, Hulland stands four-square on its village eminence in 1906, when its pews were full in an age of regular Sunday worship by all, high or lowly.

Above: Another view of Hulland Ward Gate, *circa* 1912, with the road gleaming white in late-afternoon sunshine and sun-blinds rigged on the post office windows, right foreground.

A. B. DALE,
Ironmonger
AND
Agricultural Implement Dealer,
HULLAND WARD,
Near DERBY.

Presented by

Below: Dales 's ironmonger's shop, 1909. Unchanged in appearance today, after various shop-keeping enterprises over the years it is now a beauty salon, about as far from ironmongery as you can get. *Left:* Trade card, *circa* 1910, of Anthony Beresford Dale, Frank's brother.

Right: Village ladies in their finery (those hats!) posed at the old post office; now a private house called, unsurprisingly, The Old Post Office.

Left: A leap forward to 1936: the top-heavy millinery is gone and the ubiquitous bicycles are joined by a motor-car. Otherwise, the road remains empty.

Right: A decade earlier, with the village postman striking a pose. A popular Hulland character whose name was Greatholder but was known to all as "Little Teddy Kelly". Rum, that.

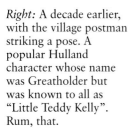

Above: Hulland's other smithy (now The Old Forge, a private dwelling) much in need of re-thatching, about 1912. Smith John Willets poses with the village bobby. John's son, also John, together with brother Ernie, carried on the trade until 1980.

Below: The Gables, Hulland Ward in 1904. The house is little changed today, but is rather less conspicuous in the streetscape than it obviously was then, being fenced on the road side, with a cluster of roofs behind and a clump of silver birches screening the front elevation.

Above: View of Ward Gate in 1933. In the foreground is the saddlery, with saddler and harness-maker Harry Harvey Dale standing outside. Beyond is the Nag's Head.

Above: The Meynell Hunt regroups near the Black Horse in this 1920s photograph. The Hunt is still to be seen around Hulland, Biggin and Kirk Ireton.

Above: View of Christ Church from "Morley Lake", Hulland Ward. Dog Lane opens to the right.

Above: The lone ash tree, long since felled, on the bend in Dog Lane below the school and church in the background.

Hulland and district has more than its share of large country houses; a plethora of houses, halls and Granges of varying periods and styles. Some are pictured here...

Above: Hulland Hall, Hulland village. Built in 1777, this typical Georgian redbrick house was much altered and enlarged in mid-Victorian style. An attractive view from the rose-garden in bright sunshine. (Photograph: Derbyshire Countryside).

Right: Another view of Hulland Hall taken in 1910, but little changed today.

Above: Hulland, Old Hall, an appealing small Elizabethan manor house, stands on its 7 acres of ground facing The Green on the edge of Hulland village. Recently occupied by the well-known local Sevier family, it is said to have been built with stone from the ruined moated manor house of the Bradbournes of Hulland Moss.

Above: This quintessentially late Victorian scene depicts Hulland Grange in the first summer of the new century. The horsewoman is Miss Annie Beardmore, a Dale cousin.

HULLAND, DERBYSHIRE.

VALUABLE RESIDENCE AND LAND,

To be Sold by Auction,

BY MR. H. D. HOLYOAK,

AT THE GREEN MAN HOTEL, ASHBORNE,

ON FRIDAY, FEBRUARY 9TH, 1877,

At 3 o'clock in the Afternoon, in the following or such other Lots as shall be agreed upon, and subject to conditions to be then produced:

LOT 1.

All that Valuable FAMILY RESIDENCE situate at Hulland, in the County of Derby, known by the name of "Hulland Grange," containing Dining-room, Drawing-room, five Bed-rooms, and Dressing-room, Kitchen, Pantry, Dairy, and the usual offices, with the Garden, Shrubberies, Stabling for two horses, Cow-house, and Piggeries. Together with THREE CLOSES of excellent Old PAS-TURE LAND, late in the occupation of Miss Eliza Webster and her under-tenant, namely:—

						A.	R.	P.
Counterflatts	...	...	...	...	...	4	0	32
Ditto	...	...	...	...	...	1	2	27
Ditto	...	...	...	...	...	1	3	12
						7	2	31

This Lot lies in a ring fence, and adjoins the road leading from Biggin to Hulland Ward, and from Hognaston to Hulland Ward, is near to Hulland Church, and is distant from Ashborne about five miles, and about two miles from the Shottle Station on the Midland Railway. The house is well adapted for a gentleman's residence.

The Tithe payable in respect of this Lot is 4s. 3½d. to the Vicar of Ashborne, and 7s. 4d. to the Appropriator.

LOT 2.

All those two closes of excellent PASTURE LAND adjoining the last Lot, and lying between the roads leading from Biggin to Hulland Ward, and from Hognaston to Hulland Ward, in the occupation of Mr. John Webster, namely:—

					A.	R.	P.
Counterflatts	...	...	...	...	3	1	3
Ditto	...	...	...	...	3	2	18
					6	3	21

The Tithe payable in respect of this Lot is 3s. 10½d. to the Vicar of Ashborne, and 6s. 8d. to the Appropriator.

Both Lots are Copyhold of the Manor of Duffield.

Mr. John Webster, of Biggin, will show the property, and for further particulars apply to Mr. JAMES NUTTALL, Derby-road, Ashborne; or at the Office of

MESSRS. WISE & SON, SOLICITORS, ASHBORNE.

Ashborne, 26 Jan., 1877.

"Well adapted for a gentleman's residence" – handbill announcing the sale by auction of Hulland Grange in 1877, when it first came into the possession of the Dale family. The vendor was the original builder of the Grange, Miss Eliza Webster.

Above: Close neighbour to Hulland Grange, a little further down Hoonwell Lane at the junction with Moss Lane, stands Biggin Grange, residence of the Coleman family. A handsome red-brick Georgian house with extensive stabling, it has been lovingly preserved, inside and out.

HULLAND, HULLAND WARD,
INTAKES AND BIGGIN.

♦♦♦♦♦♦♦

Coronation of King Edward VII.

JUNE 26TH, 1902.

♦♦♦♦♦♦♦

FAMILY TICKET.

Mr Dale & Family

Above: The Dale family was honoured with an invitation to the coronation of King Edward VII at Westminster Abbey. This monochrome reproduction of the invitation card does not do justice to the imposing original, resplendent in scarlet, royal blue and gilt.

Above: This photograph was taken in the 1970s and depicts the handsome, compact house which faces Hulland Green from the north side of the Ashbourne road. It dates from the early 18th century and is called, rather prosaically, The Green, but it used to be called "Longlands". The abutting ivy-clad cottage incorporating a stable archway dates from the 14th century and is thought to be the oldest surviving building in Hulland. The house backs onto eight acres and is currently the home of Hulland Nurseries.

Above: A village wedding, circa 1930. The bride is Doris Sims, daughter of Mr John Sims, verger and Mrs Annie Sims, school caretaker; the groom is Les Hollingworth, bus conductor. The officiating clergyman, seated extreme right of the front row, is Rev C. Baggs who succeeded Rev Dannant to the incumbency. The group is posed in the grounds of Church Cottage on Dog Lane immediately opposite the church gates; now a farmhouse.

This large wedding party is ingeniously marshalled by the professional photographer: front row seated; second row standing; third row standing on chairs and back row perched on - what?... step-ladders? scaffolding?

Left: The old common well off the north side of the main road which fell into disuse and was capped soon after mains water arrived in 1935. Its precise location passed from communal memory in a remarkably few years; especially as, it seems, a Dr Langdon of Bradley, an archaeologist, had recently excavated the site and uncovered Roman artefacts. It was rediscovered in 1986 by a dismayed householder on the estate when he dug footings for an extension and found he had a gushing spring in his back garden. The identity of the village swain draped across the coping in this snap is not known: perhaps a 70 year-old Hulland Wardean recognises himself?

Just off to the west of Hulland village is the area known as The Moss, a 6½ acre tract of boggy land in which the mediaeval fish ponds (see following page) are located. This small area was designated in 1981 an SSSI (Site of Special Scientific Interest). This measure was taken because in preceding years changes in agricultural practice together with improved drainage was causing The Moss to revert from lowland bog and heather – a rare habitat in Derbyshire – to scrub.

This trend was reversed over a period of four years by sustained clearance work carried out by volunteers under the aegis of English Nature, resulting in the regeneration of heather, sphagnum moss and a variety of marsh plants, flowers and ferns. Today, Hulland Moss, with its returning wetland species of flora, insects and small, marsh-loving trees such as grey willow, alder and birch, is once again a Mecca for botanists from near and far.

Left: A view of part of Hulland Moss, restored and reverting to lowland bog, carpeted with heather and sphagnum among its small boggy pools.

Right: A clump of sphagnum moss, one of many which are gradually spreading over the Moss's floor.

Above: This charming sylvan scene shows the Fish Ponds at Hulland Moss about 1910. The ponds would have been stocked with fish for Friday fasting by the Bradbourne family, the site of whose moated grange is nearby. *Below:* The fish ponds today, recently restored with the rest of Hulland Moss by volunteer conservators.

Above: A turn-of-the-century photograph of the old Primitive Methodist chapel at Hulland Moss, built in 1821.

Below: The old chapel today, still very much a live place of worship with services held there every Sunday. The little building is likely to remain so in the future, supported as it is by the Hulland Ladies Chapel Fellowship.

In 1987, Hulland chapel's Victorian pedal-powered harmonium was replaced by a modern electric organ. Here is the old instrument being ceremoniously. and harmoniously (ouch!), transported to its new home in Viewdales Close, where Mr and Mrs Holburn have given it house-room. Mr Gerald Redfern on the keyboard and Mr George Spencer on the tractor.

The village's involvement with, and contribution to, the bloody shambles of 1914-18 is confined to the seven names on its war memorial. The Second World War had more impact on village life, with its men enlisted in the local Home Guard platoon ("Dad's Army"), ARP (Air Raid Precautions), salvage drives and other Home Front activities. Hulland was, of course, comfortably remote from any likely Luftwaffe target – though one dark night a stray bomber did deposit a stick of incendiaries on a sand pit at Hulland Gravel's quarry site. This was thoughtful of the Hun as sand, loose or in bags, was the official counter-measure to incendiary bombs. Also, a land-mine descended on Idridgehay, close enough to rattle windows in Hulland Ward. As in most other towns and villages, the blackout caused more casualties than enemy action. Evelyn Willetts' mother was run over and killed one dark night while walking along the main road to visit her daughter and there were other road-accident victims.

The village warmly welcomed a small group of evacuee children from Manchester who were billeted in various village homes. With Hulland school at capacity, an extempore schoolroom was found for them in Hulland Hall stables under their own teacher, Miss Burton. Unfortunately, no photograph of this forlorn little band survives.

Other strangers washed up on the tide of war were a group of RAF Hurricane pilots, including many Czechs, of No 111 Squadron. The Hulland Ward connection came about when the whole squadron was "adopted" for the duration by Mr Ernest Wheatcroft, managing director of Hulland Gravel, and his wife. They had met the fliers at the funeral of sergeant pilot Alfred Gregory of Hulland Hall, killed in action with the squadron on July 23rd 1941, aged 24. Alf is buried with his parents in the churchyard and commemorated on a tablet in church. Throughout the war the 111 pilots enjoyed open house at the Wheatcroft residence, Hulland House, during their "stand-down" periods. Their favoured local watering-hole was the Black Horse, from whence they would emerge at closing-time to weave their way up the road to Highfield House, then the official billet of the CO of RAF Ashbourne, where they would be welcomed within to resume their tactical studies far into the night.

Trophy presented to Mr Ernest Wheatcroft at the end of the war by the Czech pilots 111 Squadron in gratitude for his hospitality, depicting a model Spitfire about to land at Prague on a map of their native land. It is made from the metal of a German Heinkel shot down by them during a raid on England, and is now in the possession of Ernest's son Gordon.

Below: September 1939 and the outbreak of war saw the establishment of this Observer Corps post, situated on the right of the main road at the top of the village just before the Dog Lane junction. In this picture the post is fully manned and cleared for action, with tin-helmeted heads visible, as is the

spotting-sight telescope pointing skywards. The Observer Corps, later to be dignified with the "Royal" prefix, was a kind of "Dad's Army" with headsets and binoculars, whose task was to spot and report the approach of enemy aircraft to a central control room. Among local volunteers manning the post were Harry Dale and his brother Frank, Alfred Sevier, Harold Basset and P. Smithers. The post had, of course, to be manned in all weathers *(Opposite top)*

Below: Another, rather more substantial spotting post, this one overlooking the Scow Brook Valley, which now lies under the water of Carsington reservoir. It was an observation post for spotting the fall of bombs on a practice range; a number of dummy bombs were found during reservoir excavations. Far now from its wartime role, it is a well-known landmark on the reservoir shore and is much used by birdwatchers.

In May 1940, with the war news worsening and the fall of France only weeks away, the call went out for men aged 17 to 65 not already in military service to enlist in defence of their country. Police stations were immediately swamped with volunteers from all walks of life. A nationwide organisation was set up, with volunteers formed into locally-based platoons and battalions, their main role being to guard militarily sensitive installations like power stations, gasworks and railway sidings and to keep a lookout, after Dunkirk, for enemy parachutists. This scratch force was initially called Local Defence Volunteers (soon changed to Home Guard) and its members were issued with a certificate of enrolment and a canvas armband with the letters "LDV". Uniforms came later and weapons, much later. The Home Guard was not stood down until December 1944.

(The author, as a young boy, was staying at a Muggington farm in the summer of 1940. The farmer and his two sons took their turn on night patrols, armed with their shotguns. Their Section HQ was a wooden hut high up off Muggington Lane, with a good view across the valley to Belper and beyond. Though as yet they had no officially-issued weaponry, they had been issued, presumably as a token of good faith, with a cardboard box containing twenty rounds of .202 rifle ammunition. This had to be handed over, checked and solemnly signed for at each change of watch.)

Above: Local Defence Volunteers receive instruction in appropriate, if perhaps a trifle optimistic, German phrases. But they are entirely in keeping with the LDV's determined fighting spirit of "take one with you". Still, they might have included "Don't shoot!"

Above: Later in the war, fully-uniformed, equipped and armed Home Guards practice capturing a quite convincing "German" parachutist – though he appears to have swastikas painted on his helmet to allay any doubt, and it looks as if his carefully-draped "parachute" is already about to be cut up, as they often were, for a girl-friend's trousseau.

The winter of 1946/7 is still remembered with a shudder by those old enough to have lived through it. Snow fell heavily in the last days of December and froze, and fell, and froze again. Hulland was cut off for six weeks under four to five feet of snow; fields and hedges were buried under 10-feet drifts, piled up by repeated northeast blizzards. Villagers dug themselves out; then with a fresh snow-storm overnight they had it all to do again. Normal services were immobilized; the baker's van set out from Hognaston but got snowbound, and people trudged out to it and helped themselves. Icicles up to three feet long hung from eaves. Farmers struggled to find and rescue their animals and bring them to shelter.

With hostilities not long ended, the wartime spirit reasserted itself in this crisis. Years afterwards, author Len Markham interviewed Mrs Betsy Allsop, then of Hulland village, for a book about Derbyshire's weather (*The Derbyshire & Nottinghamshire Weather Book,* Countryside Books,1994) and she told him:

"All the local men were called by the council to leave their jobs to help clear the roads. This was done by hand and shovels; no mechanical diggers in those days. The strong northeast, gale-force winds daily filled the roads. The men worked seven days a week for six weeks or more. Traffic was non-existent on the B-roads. The farmers were unable to get the milk collected; much was frozen in the churns, much also had to go down the drain, but we housewives had unlimited supplies of free milk which was appreciated by the workmen for plenty of hot drinks. We were walking on the tops of the hedges in many places. Younger folk trudged to Ashbourne for bread. Also the daughter of the village squire – Miss Anne Moseley – rode horseback over the fields to the Hognaston bakers and brought as much bread back as she could carry and shared it out among the villagers. Groceries usually delivered by the Co-op from Derby were left at Muggington Cock Inn for anyone to collect if possible. This was an unforgettable year. Frost on the windows of the living-room never thawed day or night even with a good open fire burning."

Mr George Briddon, farmer of Biggin, was at that time foreman on Lord Scarsdale's Kedleston estate, and well remembers that hard, fruitless labour. One icy morning well before dawn he was out with workmen from the estate, augmented by a squad of Italian POWs from Osmaston Park, charged with digging out the road from Kedleston to Muggington. This feat was achieved by late evening, when the exhausted men returned to quarters. In the small hours of the night a fresh blizzard undid all their labour, burying the road even deeper.

The big freeze held the countryside in its grip until the third week in March, when the longed-for thaw came at last. This brought its own problems, and Hulland folk must have been grateful for their village's elevated situation, as lower lying communities were inundated with melt-water and floods were widespread for weeks afterwards, prolonging the misery.

Right: Jean Redfern (nee Sims) aged 13 and lightly shod for the conditions, closely followed by little sister Joyce (5), negotiate a snowdrift walking to school, January 1947.

Below: A snowbound countryside at Cross-o'-the-Hands.

1979 was another exceptionally severe winter in Derbyshire, not excepting Hulland Ward, comparable in every respect to 1947 but not lasting quite as long. Severe blizzards hit the village in mid-February, with the customary 10-foot drifts and stranded livestock, not to mention commuters, of whom Hulland boasted quite a few by this date. The snowfall was followed, as in 1947, by extreme cold, – 16 degrees C being recorded locally.

Mr Alfred Allsop wields his shovel *(above)* to widen the passage so that, for the first time in weeks, he can get his car out onto the highway again *(right)*.

Above: Broad smiles (of relief?) for the camera before retreating indoors to a roaring fire and a singing kettle. Alfred and Betsy Allsop flanking the late Mrs Rosie Ditchfield outside the former's house in Hulland village.

The Tornado

The Derby Evening Telegraph of 9 September 1998 reported the ravages of a tornado which sprang from nowhere, as tornado do, to carve a swathe of destruction – well, damage anyway – diagonally from Bradley via Hulland and Hulland Ward to Wirksworth. The news item recorded farmer Les Scott of Deepdale, Hulland stating: "Part of my roof was lifted off, a neighbours roof was half removed and it actually split trees and removed them from the ground. We've got trees which have fallen onto sheds, tiles have been blown off and it knocked one man's trailer down and blew it 20 or 30 feet..." A Met Office spokesman confirmed that an area between Matlock and Ashbourne had been affected by a tornado. That's alright then; just as long as people hadn't dreamed the whole thing.

Actually, so local was the destruction that people not right in the tornado's path were quite unaware of it, and met reports of it with incredulity. The phenomenon occurred at lunchtime with residents of Millington Green noticing nothing out of the ordinary as the roof was torn off a substantial house a few hundred yards away at the junction of Biggin Lane with the A517 Belper road.

Above: The aftermath. Trees torn and uprooted at Deepdale, 9 September 1998. Trees were still in full leaf when the tornado struck (as they were when the famous Michael Fish Hurricane hit the south a England in 1987) which added to the arboreal casualties. But then, tornadoes don't happen in winter.

Above: The clearing begins. No doubt the resulting logs were in demand with winter approaching and wood-burning stoves very much in vogue hereabouts.

Leaving aside dramatic weather like tornados and 10-foot snow drifts, Hulland's usual lot, in common with the rest of this sodden island, is relentless rain for days, occasionally weeks on end. That is how our countryside gets to be so green, and looks so lovely in the statistically rarer sunshine. Something to remember when the fields and lanes are flooded and every ditch a roaring torrent. So there is usually plenty of mud about, and our local farmers are generous in sharing it around as they drive off their boggy fields and spread it along the public highway. Some of it can be deep, clinging and glutinous, like this patch encountered on the playing-field recently. As the wellies are reassuringly right way up, it can be assumed that their owner escaped its squelchy grip.

For provisions, villagers had the versatile little premises in Ward Gate (former saddlery, future beauty salon) during its incarnation as general store and newsagent, supplemented by the occasional shop in the front room of Wheel House referred to on page 73. In addition, various roundsmen called. Two bakers delivered from Hognaston, Steeples' and Dyke's, as did a third from Derby Co-op; the last also delivered groceries when ordered. There was no milk roundsman in Hulland Ward for the same reason that there is no wet-fish shop in Brixham. A butcher did a round, though.

Oldest residents remember an Ashbourne haberdasher called Adin, who toured the villages on a push-bike with a carrier, peddling socks, handkerchiefs, elastic and other small necessaries.

Doctors

The present smart, up-to-date medical centre behind the post office, built in 1977, houses the practice of Drs Gage, Bates and Wedgewood. Their predecessor, Hulland's general practitioner from the postwar years, was Dr Boden who, like the present practice, also had a surgery in Brailsford. He attended Hulland Ward twice-weekly, holding his surgery in the old post office. Before the last war, and during it, Hulland Ward's medical needs were met by the two Drs Hollick, father and son, and a third partner, a Dr Sadler. Their joint practice was based at a surgery housed adjacent to the Old Grammar School in Church Street, Ashbourne; currently a dental surgery. In those days, calling the doctor out to a home-visit when few had access to a telephone – usually involved sending a messenger, or a telegram.

Present-day villagers have a deservedly high opinion of their doctors' practice, its support staff and well-appointed premises. It may not be a positive pleasure, quite, to be ill in Hulland Ward, but you could do a lot worse.

Above: The old post office when it doubled as the doctor's surgery.

Two of the many panoramic views enjoyed by Hulland Ward residents from their – as an estate agent would say – elevated aspect. *Above:* From the top of Moss Lane eastwards to Belper and beyond. *Below:* Eaton Close residents enjoy this rolling vista to the northwards.

Above left: A recent photograph of Hulland House, situated just off the approach road to Charcon, formerly Hulland Gravel. The extension visible at the rear was specially built-on to accommodate the Czech fliers referred to in the wartime account on previous pages. *Above right:* A view of The Green, Hulland Ward, from the main road. In the background a corner of Hulland Hall's stable block can be seen, adorned with its small louvered turret.

Above: Aerial view of Hulland Ward looking west in 1966. Viewdale Close, named not for its aspect as may have been thought, but after the developer, Viewdale Building Company, is on the left. Opposite is Highfield Road, a block of 28 council houses built in 1950 mainly to house workers at the gravel works. Building of the estate has begun, with The Willows first to be completed. Dog Lane and the church are visible in the middle distance.

The estate stands on farmland purchased from the Blackwall estate for £20,000. The original farmhouse, now Melville Cottage, is located near the top of Moss Lane.

Right: A 1983 bird's-eye view of the top end of Hulland village, showing Hulland Hall to the right with The Green and main road bottom left.

Two more aerial views of Hulland Ward. Above from "Top End" looking east to the Black Horse, c1980. The estate is complete except for the new school, still building. Mr Alf Sims' Field Farm is at the right-hand edge of the picture. *Below:* The same date, The "Top End", showing The Old Smithy in centre of picture. The Severn Trent sub-station is just off the picture to the right.

Neatly bracketing the century covered by this book are Hulland Ward's two village halls: the original Institute built in 1900 and the splendid new Millennium Village Hall opened in 2000, after many vicissitudes.

The Hulland Ward Institute opened in 1900, on its rather cramped Ward Gate site, as a working mens' club. Its founding Committee, empanelled by deed of trust in August 1898, is a sonorous roll-call of Hulland's great and good at that date: "John Edward Paget Moseley of Hulland Hall, Lieutenant Colonel in Her Majesty's Bengal Army, retired; Robert Dale of Hulland Grange, Gentleman; Anthony Beresford Dale of Hulland Ward, saddler; William Henry Metcalfe of The Fields Farm in the Parish of Hulland, farmer; William Norman Thompson of Hulland Ward, veterinary surgeon..."

The Institute remained a working mens' club until 1925, when it was registered as a charity under a Board of Trustees and made open to the whole community for village meetings and functions, from whist drives to wedding receptions. (75 years on, Richard Ormsby, son of Rex who had purchased the building and land from the parish council, in elegiac mood as he carefully dismantled it, mused upon all the happy, and sad, occasions it must have witnessed over the years.)

The need for more spacious premises as the village's population grew had been evident for some time. The existing building was not capable of extension on its cramped site; also it was becoming increasingly dilapidated.

A Community Association was formed in 1985 to work with the parish council with the objective of establishing a community centre to replace the old Institute. Eyes were first turned toward the now-disused village school on Dog Lane, and negotiations were begun with Derbyshire Dales District Council to purchase it for the sum of £40,000, but the parish council withdrew in January 1998 due to restrictive covenants on the property.

In 1989 a private developer had ambitious plans to convert Fullwood Farm, just below The Hollow on the north side of the Ashbourne road, into a golf course together with a 300-bed hotel and leisure centre. As a sweetener – or "planning gain" as the town hall prefers to describe it – the developer would donate to the parish council, free of charge, a suitable parcel of land to accommodate a community centre (the same in fact on which the Millennium hall now stands). Planning permission for this grandiose development was granted in June 1992, but the original developer, together with various successors, pulled out and the scheme, together with the gratis building site, failed to materialise. So the parish council, led by its indomitable chairman Mr Charles ("Chuck") Hooley, whose enduring dream the new community centre was, returned to the start line (aka square one) and looked again for a suitable site. Many feelers were put out but none bore fruit; even a slice of the playing field on Moss Lane was considered, as a last resort.

As it became unlikely that the proposed development would take place, the parish council was approached by Mr Richard Marsh of Fullwood Farm, with an offer to sell the original piece of land which was to have been donated, a tract of 1.8 acres. A price was agreed and the parish had its building site. Now it only needed the funds.

This necessarily brief account cannot begin to describe the labours of Chuck Hooley, Bob Gilbert, council clerk and members in the formidable task of fundraising, as well as such matters as feasibility studies, design, costings and legal aspects; approaches to likely contributors in the shape of the Millennium Commission and the Countryside Agency; selection and hiring of an architect, quantity surveyor, structural engineer and solicitor. Even to approaching HM Customs & Excise, not notably the most accommodating of public servants, for VAT exemption on various works, fittings and equipment. This head-spinning labour occupied 3 years and 3 months from inception to highly satisfactory conclusion. The original concept of a community centre was scaled down to village hall; even so, it cost in the region of £327,000 all in, but what a magnificent village hall! Of that sum, the Millennium Commission donated half. The balance was made up with contributions from the Countryside Agency, village fundraising and the proceeds of sale of the old village hall and site.

After those years and months of sheer hard work and determination in the face of setbacks by the parish council, the actual building went up, from footings to fittings and furniture, in the 8 months from March to October 1999. As Chuck Hooley remarks, it was a dry summer!

Above: Village Institute prepared for dismantling, July 2001. Its locally-made bricks, products of the Hulland brickyard, were carefully preserved for future use. The carved mantle-stone set in the gable, reading "Hulland Ward Institute 1900" was removed to the new hall site and set in the grass beside the carpark.

Above: March, 1999. The site is levelled and work begins. The builders were Baines & Son of Derby and the architects David Lewis Associates of Eyam. It must have been a considerable relief to the parish council to see the building work actually begun after such protracted manoeuvres in getting the project off the ground, as it were; with costs, of course, mounting all the time – from a total of £210,000 in June, 1996 when negotiations began to £274,000 (builder's contract only) by April, 1999. The final cost, all found, with the fitting-out and professional fees, totalled £327,000.

The almost 2-acre site provides paved and tarmac parking for 40 cars, including four disabled spaces. The finishing touch to the new building, the attractive clock set in the north-facing gable, was presented to the village by Mr Richard Blackwall of Biggin.

Left: One comes down, another goes up... the new village hall nears completion, August 1999

Above: Keeping green the memory of the old amidst the new is the mantle-stone salvaged from the Village Institute which served the community for a hundred years, set into the grassy bank above the carpark.

Above: Millennium Village Hall Hulland Ward, October 1999.

Below: The official opening, performed by Patrick McLoughlin MP, with Charles ("Chuck") Hooley, chairman of the parish council, looking on.

Above: The newly-fitted, light and airy Main Hall ready to accommodate village functions...

...such as this one, *below*, captured here in full swing!

There are so many leisure activities in these days of increased mobility and, for most, comparative affluence for people to pursue; many of them enjoyed in family groups away from their home surroundings. It isn't an outing if you don't go out somewhere. Not many decades ago it was different; people made their own amusements (oh, that those words should appear on these pages, but what can you do?), especially in villages, where there was no cinema, theatre, or bingo hall just down the road. It was certainly true of Hulland Ward, which could have been described then, if not now, as a small village but which had not only an annual Carnival, with a Queen, but also a concert party, famed for miles around, called "The Green Linnets"! This latter enjoyed its heyday in the early 1960s when it regularly performed (songs and sketches) in villages – and towns – over a wide area, as well as on home ground. It comprised nine talented village ladies, a single brave man and Sybil ("Syb") Musgrove, its ebullient and uninhibited drummer. That's 10 ladies, then? Um, well... here's a photograph....

Above: The Green Linnets, 1962. Standing, l to r: Brenda Caldicott, Kate Flinn, Edith Hough, Jean Redfern, John Lemon, Pat Holborn, Margaret Woodward, Sylvia Preece (prod.). Seated: Sybil ("Syb") Musgrove, Nell Hodgkinson (piano), Edna Wood (piano).

Note the lovely frocks, identical and run-up, perhaps, by a dressmaking member; the pianists in a contrasting pattern. John and Syb tailored by Montagu Burton.

Hulland Carnival Queen 1953, and very nice too: Molly Sims.

Above: What a field to have to choose from; no walk-over for the judges. Standing, l to r: Beryl Twigg, Dora Watson, Elsie Johnson, Dorothy Watson, Rene Smith, Gwen Watson, Doreen Newton. (That's three Watsons there – sisters?). Seated: Eileen Booth, Heather Bayliss, Jean Smith, Molly Sims, Jean Sims, Joan Litchfield.

Below: Carnival float and Queen with her Maids of Honour. The crowning was performed by (extreme left) Mrs Donald Shields of Hulland House.

Above: In later years, when the Green Linnets were but a euphonius memory, Hulland Womens Institute formed a choir which was much in demand, their performances especially enjoyed in old people's homes in the area. This photograph of the choir, and don't they look smart, was posed in the old village hall on 23 September 1986.

Standing, l to r: Mary Holmes, Pat Holburn, Jean Redfern, Brenda Caldecott, Eileen Sheriff, Judy Budibent, Kath Horsley, Brenda Lee, Mary Woodhouse. Kneeling, l to r: Jackie Burns, Lilian Nash, Rosemary Steele, June Williams, Margaret Woodward, Edna Wood.

Below: The WI choir out of uniform and in costume for a concert party.

The Hulland Ward & District Tuesday Evergreen Club, known as "The Evergreens", was founded in April 1972. Membership was open to all over age 60, and weekly evening meetings were held in the village hall – on Tuesdays, of course – for whist drives, bingo sessions and such. Also, coach trips were arranged at frequent intervals.

This photograph shows the inauguration plaque in the village hall unveiled by Mrs Violet Sims, with chairman Bob Harris looking on. And behind Mrs Sims – isn't that.. .yes, it is! It's Syb!

There seems to be upward of a hundred names of founder-members listed on the board; clearly nothing like that number could have been from Hulland, so the "& District" must have been pretty widespread. Sad to record that the Evergreen Club was wound up a few years ago. The usual story; an ageing membership, dwindling numbers and younger members failing to appear, active 60 year olds (and older) much involved with their own hobbies and pursuits nowadays and disdaining clubs and societies they perceive as "for old folks". There was also a weekly luncheon club in the village hall until recently, run by volunteers, and also failing through a combination of falling numbers and uncompliable with Brussels diktats about kitchens.

Currently, Age Concern hold a day-care session in Hulland's new Millennium village hall twice weekly, transporting the elderly from surrounding villages and providing a cooked lunch.

Above: This is actually the Evergreens Christmas lunch 1982. L to r: Mr Percy Sims, Syb, Mr Frank Smith, Mr and Mrs(hidden)Les Allen and, the one smiling, Mrs Frances Sims (mother of Roy Russell of Hulland Ward Garage).

Below: At a special gathering at the Yew Tree Inn, Ednaston, on 16 June 1993 Hulland Ward's Mrs Jean Redfern is presented with a poppy brooch in recognition of her 46 years as a collector for the Royal British Legion Poppy Appeal. Pictured are other long-service collectors from the Brailsford area including another local lady, Mrs Maureen Whitbread of Biggin (extreme left) and Mr and Mrs Ian Slack of the Nag's Head.

Football Shield winners, 1951. The team, supporters, wives and girlfriends gather proudly for their victory photograph in the village hall. A real village occasion of the sort rarely seen nowadays – with most of the village present, it seems!

Above: Hulland Ward football team two seasons earlier, working-up to winning form in 1948. Back row, l to r: Wilf Fearn, Don Smith, Jack Holmes, Roy Johnson, Gordon Leslie, Ken Johnson. Front row, l to r: Sid Holmes, Mickey Simmons, Ivor Redfern, Bill Sims, Bill Fearn.

Above: Carrying on the tradition: the Junior League team of 1966. Back row, l to r: Alan Hall, Stephen Dale, Kevin Spenser, Neil Greatorex, Brian Woodward, Ian Spenser, Ian Simmons, Tommy Colman. *Front row, l to r:* Ian Redfern, Richard Hall, Nicholas Holburn, Tony Greatorex, Graham Holburn, Nicholas White.

Biggin

Go down past the wood bordering Hoonwell Lane, right to the bottom of this steep by-road, and you find yourself among the small, tight cluster of cottages and farm buildings which constitute Biggin – or more properly, Biggin-by-Hulland; for there is another Biggin some 16 miles to the north called Biggin-by-Hartington, and bemused motorists may sometimes be encountered about the lanes, misled by signpost and road map, looking for somewhere a long way elsewhere.

Our Biggin, deep in its hollow and feeling just the slightest bit claustrophobic to the stranger, is too small to be rated a village. Hamlet, then, or settlement; both of which sound rather Doomsday Book-ish, which Biggin-by-Hulland probably isn't; but the name seems to be rooted in the Viking *byggan,* a "dwelling-place", which seems fair enough, and some of its buildings are of respectable age. One of them is Old Farm, the residence and workshop of Richard Blackwall, clockmaker and scion of the principal landowners of the district. It was Richard who donated the handsome clock which adorns the front elevation of the new village hall and he has a large gilded clockface advertising his craft on the front wall of his own house. Old Farm was a working farm until 1968 when, like many others in the area, much of its land was parcelled out and let for grazing. There are still a few working farms in Biggin: Home Farm, next-door to Richard, farmed by the Whitbreads, and Hays Farm (Gray) a few hundred yards to the east.

There is also a chicken farm rearing battery hens, which you wouldn't know was there unless you had the misfortune to encounter in the lane the waste lorry returning from its periodic visit. Local pedestrians recognise this vehicle from a distance and take whatever evasive measures are open to them.The unwary or unknowing, stepping aside to let it pass, are overtaken by gagging, watering eyes, nausea and, fleetingly, a longing for death.

Biggin's most important building happens to be easily the finest for many miles around, though the casual visitor could pass it by unnoticed, so well screened is it by bushy hedges and tall trees. This is Biggin House, a Grade II* - listed Georgian country gentleman's residence dating from 1750. It was for most of its life the home of the Blackwall family of ancient lineage, of which more anon. As the following pictures attest, it is a gem of a country house, standing in its acre of well-tended gardens and exotic trees; smallish, as such houses go, with 23 rooms in all; prettily faced with decorative freize and pilasters in the pink-blushed sandstone from the Blackwall's own quarry. Biggin House deserves to be better known, but perhaps prefers not to be; like the rest of Biggin, seclusion seems to suit it.

Above: Biggin House, showing the semi-circular bay on the south face.

Right: Evening shadow and a setting sun bring out the pink hue of the sandstone.

Evelyn Blackwall, spinster sister of John Blackwall Evans-Backwall, lived here for many years and is remembered with affection by older villagers for her good works. Evelyn's sister Millicent was the wife of Bishop Smith of Lagos.

Summery lawns...

and wintry boughs.

Above: Cottages at the top end of Biggin. The one on the left was originally Home Farm's cowshed.

Left: A view, since obscured by trees, showing Home Farm to the left and The Old Farm on the right.

Right: The chicken farm, from a distance.

The Blackwalls of Blackwall: an old local family

In any history of the area – Hulland, Biggin, Kirk Ireton – almost as far back as you care to go, the Blackwall name will occur, with many branches of the family to be found elsewhere in Derbyshire until after the Civil War, when they paid the price for backing the wrong horse. The Blackwalls are known to have been established as minor gentry hereabouts since the early 15th century, and may go even further back in local entrenchment.

What is known is that the family seat of Blackwall Hall has occupied the same site, with Blackwalls in residence, from 1414 to the present day: almost a record among the lesser gentry of Derbyshire. (Except for a short gap in recent years, 1959-1978, when they let the Hall and retired to their other seat, Biggin House, pictured on pages 53 and 54. Mr and Mrs John Blackwall are again resident at the Hall.)

The Blackwalls, Gells and Wigleys all owned property in the Wirksworth area from an early date, and all gained substantial income from the lead-smelting which they engaged in, like many landowners in mid-Derbyshire, from the mid-16th century. They were known as "brenners".

The law, then as now, was a good racket to be in in the Middle Ages, when property and title disputes among the landed were commonplace. Robert Blackwall was a Master in Chancery when he married into the squirearchical family of Litton of Litton in 1457. Richard, his son, a serjeant at law, also married well, added to his lands and was granted a coat of arms in 1494. Thus various branches of the family waxed and prospered, until they were caught on the losing side in the Civil War. In the aftermath many local families of prominence were dispossessed and vanished from the scene, including the Knivetons of Bradley. The Kirk Ireton branch of the Blackwalls, however, survived.

In 1838 the male line "failed", to use the genealogical term, and the sole heiress, Emma Blackwall, married The Rev Charles Evans, first vicar of Christ Church, Hulland. Their son, John, named Blackwall Evans-Blackwall, adopted the surname and arms of Blackwall by Royal Licence in 1871, but his descendants dropped the "Evans".

In 1876 a compendium was published of the country's landowners. The Derbyshire section was headed by the Duke of Devonshire (of course!) and the Duke of Rutland; others following in descending order of their spread of acreage. In the "squire" category (1,000 to 3,000 acres) appear the Meynells of Meynell Langley and the Blackwalls of Blackwall. Since then of course, the family estate, like most others, is much diminished; due no doubt to the depredations of inheritance and other taxes.

Blackwall Hall, the Grade II-listed ancestral seat of the Blackwalls of Kirk Ireton, currently the home of Mr and Mrs John Blackwall. It occupies a splendid site on a southerly slope, overlooking the deep hollow containing Biggin and what was until recently their other family seat, Biggin House.

Parts of the present Hall are pre-16th century. The house is built of a mixture of ashlar and coursed rubble of local red-stained Ashover Grit (vide Maxwell Craven and Michael Stanley, *The Derbyshire Country House*). Many alterations and additions have been made over the cenuries, culminating in this attractive south elevation with its two 16th-century straight, pointed gables flanking an ornate central one which caps the roof of a central hallway built to link the east and west wings in about 1800.

Right: Emma Evans, neé Blackwall, heiress of the Blackwall estate. She married The Rev Charles Evans, Vicar of Hulland, in 1852. She is pictured with her infant son, John.

Left: A charming study of John Blackwall, father of John and Richard, dated 1913 when he was aged 5. He was known to the family as "Pat" and to others, in later life when he managed Mercaston Quarry, as "The Major".

Above: JBE Blackwall takes a turn on the lawn with Blackwall Hall behind, circa 1920. A very handsome and distinguished figure, he was a gentleman of leisure in those more prosperous days.

Above: Studio portrait of John Blackwall Evans-Blackwall (1855-1924) as a young man.

Old Farm, Biggin; residence and workshop of Richard Blackwall, clockmaker, John's younger brother. Richard made and donated the clock which enhances the front elevation of the Millennium village hall. Old Farm was a working farm until 1968, when much of its land was leased for grazing.

The reader will encounter elsewhere in this book some gentle mockery of the ubiquity of Bonnie Prince Charlie legends. Here is another, but with evidence in support of it. In 1745, year of the Young Pretender's ill-starred march on London, the mayor of Derby was one John Eaton, a relation by

Above: Old Farm in 1890.

marriage of the Blackwalls. He is said to have ferried Charles Edward across the River Derwent (he was forever crossing water) just before he thought better of it and returned whence he came. The rest is history, as they say, but Richard has in his possession a small japanned-metal snuffbox with, on the underside of the lid, a painted miniature of the young prince allegedly presented by him in gratitude to Richard's relative. A good story and probably a true one; the painting is said to be a good likeness and its being on the hidden underside of the lid is true to romantic, clandestine Jacobite tradition.

Left: Miss Evelyn Blackwall and her nephew John ("Pat") out on the lake, 1914. Evelyn later lived at Biggin House. In this study, Miss Blackwall's huge hat is balanced by a formidable chin.

Right: A family group about 1912. At rear: Evelyn and John B E-Blackwall; front: Robert, Sophie (neé Statham), Lucy (neé Eaton).

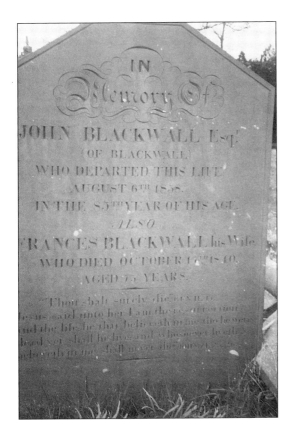

Some of the Blackwall family graves in Kirk Ireton churchyard. There are several others, including that of Charles Evans, first Vicar of Hulland, who chose to be interred with his in-laws. He has a memorial tablet in his own church.

This consists of the dozen or so houses strung out along Nether Lane, that which runs between the bottom ends of Hoonwell and Biggin Lanes (incidentally, Biggin Lane does not lead to Biggin; Hoonwell Lane does, adding to the bafflement of delivery-van drivers). A couple of these dwellings are modern – 1950s built – but most are old, with the oldest clearly shown by reference to its deeds to date from 1612. Most, again, have been much altered and added to in recent years. Half of them are, or were once, farms: Lanehead Farm, Millington Green Farm, Chapel Farm, Meadow Farm and Milner's Farm; now the private houses of, mostly, commuters. One working farm/smallholding remains; that of Mr Eric Wood, the aptly if unimaginatively-named Bungalow Farm.

Left: Nether Lane, Millington Green.

Below: Millington Green across the fields from Biggin Lane.

Above: Millington Green Farm, Nether Lane. The original part of this building is the brick range to be seen on the right, which dates from 1612, making it Millington Green's oldest.

The house next door, an attractive cottage called "Walden", was extensively rebuilt 40 years ago from an ugly and largely derelict three-storey house occupied until a few years before her death in 1977, aged 100, by Frances May Killer. It was called Chapel House and was the original meeting-house of the Biggin Strict Methodists until they moved to a purpose-built chapel up the lane (another Chapel House!) now much enlarged and in private use. There is a stone lintel above a door to the sitting room in "Walden" into which is carved *B.S.M.* 1784.

Right: Nether Lane under snow in February 1994. Chapel House to the left, Chapel Farm on the right.

Above: Aerial view of Haven Cottage, Nether Lane in 1965, when Mr Sam Sims kept a piggery there. Some years and a change of ownership later, in the late 1970s, Mrs Peggy Thompson was in the more fragrant business of serving cream teas to passing hikers and cyclists.

Below: Haven Cottage today, taken from the front; which is to say, the back.

Above: Rose Cottage, formerly Moss Cottage, is Grade II-listed, and is the second-oldest building in Millington Green. It can be reliably dated to a few years either side of 1750 because of a short-lived architectural fashion in the cutting of the window mullions. The elongated middle window of the ground floor was obviously once a doorway. Until the 1920s the property included several acres of pasture but has now just a large and well-stocked garden to the rear.

Below: From little acorns... Mrs Deakins' old barn and woodstore (see next page).

...mighty oak trees grow.

Only quicker. Two years later, and "Oak Cottage" is on the market for – well, quite a large sum.

Below: Millington Green slumbers under a blanket of snow in the winter of 1955. Nether Lane was then, and still is, frequently overlooked by the council's snow plough, and the small community was often snowed-in for days in those severer winters.

This small hole in the ground protected by an extempore grille (a shelf from somebody's fridge, it looks like) and some makeshift fencing, is Millington Green's once-famous Spa Well, an important local water source until 1954 when piped water reached Nether Lane. It is located in an overgrown corner of the field on the sharp bend at the bottom of the lane. Its water is rich in sulphur (H_2S) and was particularly popular during the war years as it had the property of making rationed tea go further. It is very pure and its temperature is constant, which indicates a deep source. Mr Ian Glover of nearby June Croft (see below) remembers regular visits to the well in the late 1940s and early 50s by a rich and health-conscious old lady's vintage Rolls Royce, with the chauffeur despatched to fill a couple of milk-churns and load them into its capacious boot.

Below: June Croft comprises two cottages; the farther one in this picture was originally called Spa Well Cottage.

In the deep dell behind Haven Cottage and its neighbours is a small wood of huge, mature beeches, that most majestic and beautiful of English trees. It is called Paradise Wood by locals, and if that name does not appear on maps, it should. A public footpath leads through it from Nether Lane, over a brook and steeply up to the fields on which Mr Donnelly grazes his prize Simmental cattle, to Moss Lane and the estate. As with all beechwoods, autumn is the best time to see it in its glory. Winter is good, too; with the fallen leaves still golden and crunching underfoot it is like walking on cornflakes, if you've ever done that (which you will have if you've had children).

Chapter 2 – Village Inns

At the beginning of the last century there were four public houses within the parish; today there are two. This reflects a national trend, at least in rural areas, for "the local" to close down and is probably due more to drink-drive laws than to a diminution in pub-going, as distinct from church-going. Also, in Hulland Ward's case, the old inns began life as coaching houses, a trade which had disappeared by the 1860s with the spread of railways.

The village is luckier than most of its size in retaining two; it very nearly didn't…

Above: Straddling the parish boundary to the west is "the pub with two names", the Jinglers. If you were heading for Ashbourne, that is – on your way home it was the Fox and Hounds. (Was, sadly: at the time of writing it is closed and for sale as a private dwelling). The story has it that the premises, bisected by the boundary, was licensed in both parishes under the separate names, one with closing time half an hour later than the other, so customers could move to the back room to continue drinking legally. That's the story, anyway. The inn was once a toll-house, and this 1960s sketch shows the board, since removed, listing the toll charges for goods and vehicles using the Belper road. This inn was probably originally built on a cross roads, the more important road being not the current road to Ashbourne, but a road at the side leading into the Peak District.

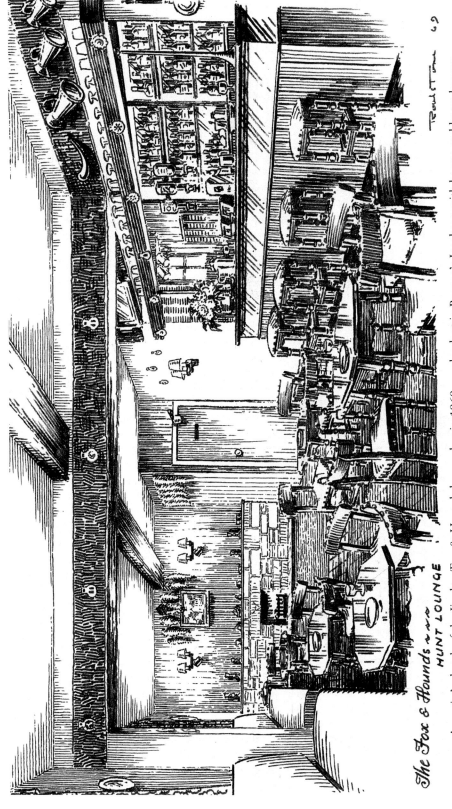

The Fox & Hounds ~~
HUNT LOUNGE

An artist's sketch of the Jinglers/Fox & Hounds lounge bar in 1969, resplendent in Brewer's Jacobean with beams and horse-brasses.

Below: The Black Horse Inn in 1912. Note the two boxed-in well pumps at the front – no piped water supply in Hulland Ward until 1935. The Black Horse is the oldest of Hulland's inns, dating to at least the late 18th century, possibly earlier. It was originally a coaching posthouse for travellers to and from the north.

Given its long history, it is difficult to believe that quite recently – 1995, in fact – it came within a whisker of being bulldozed to build a dozen houses on the site. It was saved by outraged villagers, led by the parish council who petitioned the then Heritage Secretary. In support of their case, and introducing thereby a felicitous note of farce to the proceedings, they innocently quoted a farrago of historical codswallop about the inn lifted directly from the landlord's own menu cards, claiming connection with, among others, Bonnie Prince Charlie. They were apparently unaware of a pub landlord's predeliction for inventing hauntings, Bonnie Prince Charlies etc to attract the gullible to their premises. The licensee, seeing his own colourful interpretation of history about to be used against him, hastily confessed to embroidering the facts a little: but it didn't affect the outcome, fortunately, and this ancient inn still enhances the village scene.

Above: The old Nag's Head inn pictured in 1908, a year before it was demolished. The brewer's dray indicates delivery-day, with the empties ready for collection. "That's Granddad Booth with the horse and trap", says Evelyn Willets.

Below: The new Nag's Head stands on the site of its predecessor in 1910, soon after it was built.

Above: Wheel Inn, Hulland Ward, as it looked in 1907, when already a hundred years old, and...

Below: The present Wheel House, with little external evidence of the original building; though older residents recall what is now the sittingroom being the venue of village dances. Also remembered is a little shop in the front room 30 or 40 years ago.

At the beginning of the last century there were a total of 88 farms and smallholdings in the combined townships of Hulland, Hulland Ward and Biggin. There are many fewer today; unsurprisingly, given the hard work, long hours and low returns which are the common lot of the small farmer.

Then as now, most Hulland farmland was pasture, for the grazing of beef and dairy cattle. There was some arable, growing corn and root crops, a few sheep and some pig-keeping. Arable farming was labour-intensive in the days before tractors and combine harvesters and at harvest-time casual labourers were employed, notably the gangs of Irish itinerants "fondly" recalled by older Hulland farmers. Farming was hard labour for men and horses – those huge, majestic shire horses everywhere to be seen in those days: pulling ploughs and seed drills, mowing hay and corn, hauling mangels and spreading muck. Hulland's smiths and harness maker never lacked work for hand and eye. But the district was mainly one of livestock farming – except for the war years, when government in the guise of War Agricultural Committees directed farmers to plough up their pastures and grow wheat, oats, barley and potatoes, often on unsuitable soil; but they were desperate days. Most of it reverted to grass after the war.

In recent years many local farms have been broken up, with the land disposed of in penny packets; some for building on, most sold or rented to neighbouring farms and smallholdings, with the effect – particularly noticeable at haymaking and silage-cutting time – of farmers ranging far and wide to their scattered fields.

Above: There are a number of prize herds in the area. This magnificent Simmental heifer, bred by Mr D M Donnelly of Atlow House, Moss Lane, Hulland Ward, wears her winner's rosette at the Royal Show in July 1990. *(Photo by Genus)*

Above: A view of Stony Cliff Farm at about the time it was purchased by Hulland Gravel, to whose premises it lay adjacent. The company demolished the farm in 1982, and incorporated the site in their premises.

Right: When still a going concern, Stony Cliff's farming brothers Arthur Bernard Hall (left) and Eric Hall, take a breather from stacking straw.

A Typical Farm of the Area

Mansell Park Farm lies two miles south of Hulland Ward, mid-way between it and Brailsford. It was worked by generations of the Hall family, most recently by Mr Phil Hall, now of Intakes Lane. When farmed by Phil's father Frank, it had 124 acres and sustained a dairy herd of 20 milking cows. In addition, according to an article in the *Derbyshire Advertiser* of April 21, 1911 there were:

"eight in-calf heifers and eight yearlings. All the milk is sent to Nestles factory at Brailsford. A good number of calves are reared, but as all the milk is sold off, no pigs are kept. The land comprising the farm is very rich and exceedingly well-kept; in fact everything in the place is in perfect order, for Mr Hall believes in paying attention to the most minute details".

This must have made gratifying reading for Frank; also the mention of his breeding shire horses from his prize stallion "Rickford Crown Prince", which according to the article, "is a black, standing fully 17 hands, and was commended in London. He has short legs, with a great abundance of hair, measuring twelve inches of good flat bone beneath the knee..."

Above: Mr Frank Hall in working clothes, poses proudly with one of his famed shire horses. Could this be the prize stallion Rickford Crown Prince? And if so, did he have to work as well?

Right: Some years later, in 1950, and semi-retired, Frank, in his best suit, eagerly awaits his transport for a day at Derby Market.

Below: A young Phil Hall shares a tractor seat with Jean Lytle in the Mansell Park yard in 1948. Jean (later Mrs Sam Sims) was a Womens Land Army girl who found she enjoyed life on the farm and returned to it after the war. WLA girls were employed on many Hulland and Biggin farms. Mrs Margaret Milewski(neé Hind) at Derbyhill Farm, Cross-o'-the-Hands, still living in the house where she was born, remembers two Timber Corps girls billeted on her parents during the war, tree-felling in the quaintly-named Holgate's Carr copse behind the farm.

Dick Murfin was a farmhand at Mansell Park and a veteran of the First World War who had lost an arm in the trenches. He wore a steel hook in place of his missing hand which was no handicap – quite the reverse – in performing the full range of jobs on the farm. Here (right) he takes a refresher during the thirsty work of hedgelaying in company with the Hall children Peter, Philip and Margaret; and, (below) thatching a stack, when the hook must have been useful.

Above left: Mrs Eleanor Hall, Phil's mother, broke-in young horses as a sideline. She is pictured here astride one of Mr Alfred Sevier's hunters. *Above right:* Little Margaret Hall, aged 4, poses fetchingly at Mansell Park.

Below: A literary connection to a Hulland farm: on the left of this trio of 1930s ladies is Mrs Frances Gerrard (widow of Philip Gerrard senior of Bricklands Farm), the last surviving second cousin of "George Eliot" (Mary Anne Evans) the novelist and author of *Adam Bede, The Mill on the Floss, Silas Marner* etc: most of whose works had Midlands farms for their settings.

Above: Another local farm now no more. This was Crossways Farm – confusingly, one of three of that name in the parish – which was located at "Bottom End" near the triangle, and was the home of the Naylor family. This photograph dates from 1964, not long before the farmhouse was demolished.

Below left: Proud parent (1). Mrs Naylor at the farmhouse door with her youngest, two year-old John.
Below right: Proud parent (2). Dolly the cow with her new-born triplets. A rare event; well done, Dolly!

Left: A young David Hough, already one for the girls, at Crossways in 1948, with (l to r:) Joyce Naylor, Joyce Sims and Margaret Naylor.

Left: Windmill Farm, high up on Biggin Lane, photographed from "Walden" 's back garden.

For many years, a vital service to the local farming community was provided by Jacksons the threshers of Newhouse Farm, later of Spring Hill, Hulland Ward. "John Jackson, threshing machine proprietor" is listed in *Bulmer's History & Directory of Derbyshire* of 1895, but the firm was older than that, for the John Jackson listed was the son of the founder, Samuel. Farmers within a 5-mile radius availed themselves of the service, with "everyone mucking in" at the busy harvest time when Jackson's traction engine and threshing machine must have been a familiar sight in the area as it trundled ponderously, and noisily, from farm to farm. The traction engine found plenty of employment at other times of year: winter sawing and logging, and as workhorse for any heavy haulage job. The firm ceased operations in the early 1950s as arable farming in the region declined and the first combine harvesters appeared.

Above: An early (1905) line-up of a threshing gang, with the boss, John Jackson in the centre of the group. The agricultural threshing machine was early, basic technology; a large wooden box on wheels, festooned with belts and pulleys – see how little changed later models are in the following photographs...

In 1892 John Jackson left Newhouse Farm off Biggin Lane for newly-built premises, a half-mile east of Hulland Ward just off the Belper road, which he named Spring Hill (now Springhill Farm). These pictures show his traction engine at work felling and sawing mature trees to supply timbers for the new house. Note, in the picture below, a sawmill driven by belt from the engine.

Above and below: Spring Hill – hauling stone and excavating the footings. Those old workmen sport a variety of headgear, from the battered top hat of the man standing beside the chute, above, to a bowler-hatted figure, below, with his hands in his pockets: an idle onlooker or, possibly, the architect...? Unlike modern buildings, with their mass-produced components, all the necessary materials for Spring Hill – stone, timber and bricks – were from local sources.

On with the threshing, two photographs from the 1920s.

Above: A crew pause in their labours
to pose for this 1940s photograph.

Right: threshing in the late 1940s,
the last such activities before
Jackson's ceased operating in
1952.

Above: This machine gets a ride on a low loader, about 1948. Left to right: John Jackson jun., Arthur Wain, Walter Booth. *Below:* Threshing machine has a driving belt replaced, 1950.

Above left: Brickhills Farm, Smith-hall Lane, as it was in the 1930s, and... *Above right:* As it is today, no longer a farmhouse, and much altered and enlarged.

High summer at Mansell Park, August 1947 (below). Bill Salt and Sydney Gerrard stook corn sheaves in the traditional way. Sydney Gerrard was Mrs Frank Hall's half-brother. Bill's mother was the Mrs Salt who kept the post office at Hulland Ward. He and his family now farm at Abney, near Hathersage.

Above: A recent colourful addition to the Hulland scene is the spectacular Four Shires bloodhound pack kennelled at Newhouse Farm, Biggin Lane. As a drag hunt, one which hunts a human quarry, it escapes the obloquy which at present surrounds fox-hunting, while enjoying all the panoply and glamour of the latter, including huntsmen in pink. Here they take to the fields led by Joint Master Mr Edward Hammond. Left is Mrs Naomi Hammond with huntsman Mark Knight on the right.

Below: Another shot of the pack. They make a stirring sight, loping through the narrow Biggin lanes on their morning run – two dozen identical (to the untrained eyes) huge hounds *silently* flowing like a chocolate-brown stream between the hedgerows, a horseman before and behind and most days, an elderly lolloping black labrador gamely bringing up the rear.

Newhouse Farm, home of the pack, lies deep in its hollow off Biggin Lane. Until recently, the pack had not had an outing for almost a year due to the blanket ban following the foot and mouth epidemic, but enjoyed a chase on Boxing Day 2001 after a partial lifting of restrictions. Normally the pack hunts three times a fortnight during the season October to March, within a radius of 25 miles from home; with the prior agreement of farmers and landowners in the area selected. The human quarry are experienced cross-country runners with orienteering skills; necessarily fit young men – or women: one of the hunt's best quarries is a young woman who has been running for the past five years. Mr Hammond emphasizes that his pack are not draghounds, which, he says, are "failed foxhounds" – his dogs are bloodhounds which track human scent alone, without the aid of the aniseed-soaked rag which the former's quarry must carry.

The pack came to Hulland from Tenbury Wells in Worcestershire, where they were known as the Kyre Bloodhounds.

Below: "Roses round my door" - Brick Kiln Farm, Hulland Ward. Its charming cottage garden abloom in full summer sunlight.

Above: Keeping the tradition alive – Mr George Briddon, well-known Biggin farmer, competing in a ploughing match and probably winning; he usually did. Just look at those furrows!

Considering the current pressures on working farmers, it is remarkable that not more local farms have disappeared. Hulland farmers are a doughty, dogged breed representing, as small farmers, probably the last truly independent-minded people in this country; committed to their land and livestock following, in many cases, generations of their families on the same farm. It is thanks to them that Hulland Ward still overlooks a traditional landscape: a neat landscape with pasture, trees and trimmed hedges intact, unchanged for two hundred years and more. Let us be thankful and hope that it may last for many more.

Chapter 4 – Heart of the Village: Christ Church, Hulland

Hulland's plain little parish church stands four-square on the highest point in the parish, embowered in its screen of tall, arching lime trees. Beauty, they say, is in the eye of the beholder, a truism which applies as much to architecture as to most things. Christ Church, Hulland is not likely to be found on those lists of ancient and beautiful parish churches commended as worthy of a visit by devotees of such buildings but, constructed in the year 1838 of uncompromising sandstone blocks with a squat, embattled tower at its western end, its very plainness is appealing, some say. The churchyard, twice extended during the past century, with extensive and windswept views of rolling countryside far away to the west, is scattered with the headstones of Hulland's oldest and once most numerous families: Allcocks, Fearns, Dales, Hoons and Gregorys among others, with a cluster of Bainbrigges in an honoured place near the porch.

Austere and "low church" within as well as without for most of its life, until a new chancel with its blaze of stained glass was added in 1961, the interior, as a former Vicar observed, was "rather like that of a preaching-house". It is true that, rectangular, chastely unadorned and with a "chapel"-style gallery above the porch, the ambience is more Nonconformist than Anglican. Not so the observance, though.

Plain but dignified then, like its congregation (spiritually, that is!). And it is, after all, the congregation which constitutes and defines a church, rather than the fabric. From the day of its consecration until the postwar years, the church was at the hub of village affairs. In common with congregations almost everywhere, recent times have seen a reduction in regular churchgoing among Hulland folk; the remaining faithful, though, have kept Christ Church a living – and lively! – institution, as the following pages reveal.

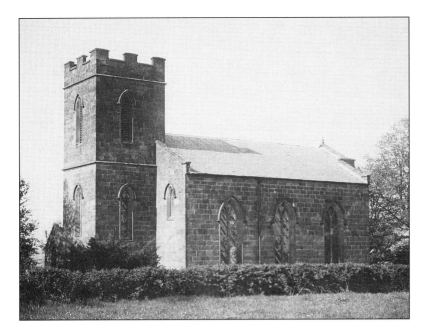

Left: View of the south aspect of Hulland church about 1910. It is essentially unchanged since its building some 60 years earlier.

Below: A similar view post-1961, with the new chancel built-on. The chancel was dedicated on June 22nd of that year by the Bishop of Derby, Rt Rev Geoffrey Allen. It took a year to build and cost nearly £4,000. The money was donated by two brothers, members of the Borough family which had associations with Hulland Ward going back to the days of Charles II. They were Mr Reginald Borough of Market Lavington in Wiltshire and the Rev Roland Borough, a former Vicar of Bradbourne, of Belper Road, Derby.

In a newspaper interview (*Derbyshire Advertiser June 23 1961*) Rev Roland Borough said they wanted to give a new chancel because Hulland had been the home of his family for so long, and that extension on the east side gave the church "a far better appearance". Few would argue with that.

Two views of The Old Vicarage,
Hulland Ward, in the 1920s. Typical
of the big, rambling residences with
stables and coach-house attached.
These were provided by the
Victorian church for its incumbents
in an age of large clerical families,
ready availability of domestic
servants and the perceived
requirement to house the clergy in a
style befitting their standing in the
community. Few of them still serve
their original purpose today, given
the cost of heating and maintaining
them, even without servants!

Right: Today's Hulland Vicarage is a
modern house on the estate; less
imposing but enjoying all mod.con.,
with the Vicar dwelling very much
among his flock. The Old Vicarage is
now a private house.

Above: The churchyard gates, opening on to quaintly-named Dog Lane. This was according to local folklore "Dog Lanes", originating some time after the 14th century when the whole area formed part of the royal forest of Duffield Frith and the king's hunting dogs were kept here. Just beside the gates stands the parish war memorial (top right). It was unveiled on March 15th 1920 by Admiral Sir Frederick Inglefield, living in retirement at Windley. No Beatty or Jellicoe, this obscure admiral's name was to outlast theirs in Royal Naval renown as he, a Signals specialist, had invented a little bronze quick-release gadget for signal-flag halliards still in use 80 years later and known as the Inglefield Clip.

The war memorial bears the names of seven Hulland men who gave their lives in the First World War while three who died in the Second are remembered on a plaque in the church *(left);* a close approximation to the casualty rates of the two conflicts.

Above left: Reverend William Dannant, the charismatic and much-loved Vicar of Hulland from 1911 to 1928 poses with Mrs Dannant at the Vicarage porch. Lengthy incumbencies were commoner then than today, though Rev Dannant's 17 years in post are eclipsed by the tenure of his predecessor Rev Robert Leighton Barnett, 1876 to 1911. *Above right:* A picture of Victorian domestic rectitude – Bishop Alfred Smith and his wife at Hulland Vicarage in 1919. Bishop Smith (of Lagos) was a close friend of Rev Dannant and would spend part of his home furlough at the Vicarage, often preaching the Sunday sermon in church. As young men, both clergymen had been keen on missionary work but Rev Dannant's health unfortunately precluded it (though darkest Africa's loss was Hulland's gain); his friend entered the field, where his labours were rewarded with a colonial bishopric. Bishop Smith's wife Millicent, pictured here, was a Blackwall; sister to Evelyn of Biggin House.

Opposite: This group photograph of the parochial church council (PCC) was taken on the occasion of Rev Dannatt's retirement at Easter 1928 and includes many prominent villagers of that date. Back row, l to r: Mr F Graham, headmaster Hulland school; Jack Sims (of the cycle shop), sidesman; John Willetts (blacksmith), sidesman; Harry Harvey Dale, John Sims, verger; George Lee, sidesman.

Middle, l to r: Mrs Mary Taylor (mother of Evelyn) of The Moss, Hulland village; Mrs Thursa Dale of Hulland Grange (wife of Harry Harvey); Mrs Ted Gregory of Old Hall; Mrs Rosetta Nash; Miss Evelyn Blackwall, of Biggin House; Mrs Annie Sims, school caretaker; Mrs George Lee; the Misses Wright and Bonshor, teachers at the village school.

Front, l to r: Mr Arthur Easter, cobbler and organist; Mr Ted Gregory of Old Hall, churchwarden; Rev Dannatt and Mrs Jean Dannatt; Mr Joe Barton, churchwarden; Mr Joe Maskery, farmer of Biggin and Mr Albert Nash, sidesman.

Miss Bonsher, the young schoolteacher, lodged with the Lees until she married Jack Sims. They were the days when Cherry Blossom Boot Polish was a blue-chip investment.

Above: A more recent church occasion: a Musical Evening in 1995. The Cubs and Brownies were much involved and are pictured here with their leaders. Extreme left back row is Martin Davis, organist and musical director; while below him on the left, in light coloured shirt, is Graham Lee, an accomplished brass-player. Centre of back row, in golden bowler and revolving bow tie is the previous Vicar, Rev Richard Smith.

Right: Fund-raising has to be a constant preoccupation of church members these days, with the straitened financial circumstances of the C of E necessitating an annual contribution from individual churches to central funds: the controversial "parish share". In addition, normal running costs have to be met – heating and lighting, churchyard maintenance, insurance etc, and above all, building repairs.

   An ever-popular means of fund raising and always a "good little earner" is the church cake stall *(Right).* Especially when pitched as here, given a fine day, on a footpath alongside the churchyard to catch the eye of passing Carsington Water visitors as well as the locals who know how delicious these cakes invariably are. So you have to arrive early to

avoid disappointment. The record – so far – for clearing a bench laden with fresh-baked, scrumptious cakes and buns, leaving only the tablecloth and a few crumbs, is 35 minutes!

Left: Church fairs (often spelt "fayres", regrettably) held in the summer and at Christmas can be useful money-spinners but involve weeks of hard work on the part of the organisers and depend for a reasonable profit on the generosity of of donors of raffle and treasure hunt prizes. Here is "Stack the Parcels" in progress, with rapt onlookers but not a protruding tongue in sight.

In common with all parish churches, maintenance and repair of the fabric within and without is a constant drain on funds. When damp began attacking the walls of Christ Church in 1990, damp-proofing became necessary. This was a costly job for the professionals, but several hundred pounds was saved by parishioners rallying round to do the necessary making good and re-decorating afterwards. Painting began in the chancel after the heavy box-pews had been unscrewed and man-handled out of the way. Several weeks and many gallons of emulsion later (not all of it confined to walls and ceiling!) the job was done; pews hauled back into place, a thorough cleaning and Hulland's parish church, damp-proofed and pristine, was back in business. Unfortunately, at the time of writing, a recent survey has established that the building needs £50,000-worth of repairs and modification. Dedicated and resourceful as they are, it is hard to see how such a staggeringly huge sum can be raised by the congregation alone, and the future of Christ Church is in question for the first time in its 164-year history.

Right: The chancel ceiling gets an extra-thick coat to cover the cracks. Willing and eager to help as people were, up to shoulder level, there was an understandable reluctance among the more mature of the congregation to mount ladders and rickety scaffolding to reach the soaring heights. It was necessary to co-opt a husband who had been a jolly Jack Tar in the dim past, who could not therefore deny having a head for them, to deal with the ceiling and upper walls, though his trembling while aloft accounted for much of the splashed paint.

Below: The youngest member of the congregation, little James Crossland, enjoys the end result.

To mark Christ Church's 150th anniversary in 1988, the church was decorated throughout by talented lady members with flowers and foliage in individual arrangements with the Psalms as a theme, making a breath-taking display.

Above: The previous Vicar of Hulland, the Rev Richard Smith, and his wife Jane. Richard was Vicar from 1985 to 1996. Jane is not wearing Vicar's wife's working dress in this shot; she is on her way to a wedding.

To mark Millennium Year the church staged a Flower Festival in the summer. Such festivals have become popular among parishes recently, but this was the first held at Christ Church. The set-pieces, on Biblical themes, were breathtaking, and had to be seen to be believed; artistry, imagination and skill transforming the whole church into a blaze of light and rich colour. So successful was it that it was extended to a second week by popular request. A few of the displays are reproduced here; in monochrome, unfortunately, so you must imagine the riot of colour. The very talented arrangers are not cited here, but they know who they are!

Left: The three Kings.

Below: The Angel Gabriel; *opposite top left:* Joseph's Coat of Many Colours; *opposite top right:* Jacob's Ladder.

Proud and happy with the task completed, one of the arrangers poses amidst a colleague's successful set-piece.

"When the voices of children are heard on the green, and laughing is heard on the hill", as the poet put it, and it would be a sad and lifeless community lacking those sounds. Not that Hulland Ward is at any risk of falling into that category: the primary school roll stands at 87 at the time of writing. The number is fairly stable despite falling birth rates nationally, all too often resulting in closure of schools, particularly rural ones. Such was the fate, due to falling rolls, of the village school in neighbouring Hognaston a decade ago. Hulland Ward is fortunate in that respect, with its middle-aged and retired population balanced by numerous young families, particularly on the estate. Fortunate, too, in the quality of its parenting, if the relative absence of vandalism and other anti-social behaviour around the village is anything to go by, and if it is not patronising to say so. This in spite of the undeniable fact that, in common with most rural places, there is little enough for the young to do outside school hours. Until recently there had been an active youth club; perhaps there soon will be again, in the splendid new village hall. Meantime, in spite of some difficulty in recruiting and retaining leaders, the Hulland Scouts and Beavers continue to flourish, as subsequent pages reveal...

The School

The original Hulland Church of England school was opened on Dog Lane, beside the parish church, in 1863, shortly before the Education Act of 1870 made elementary schooling compulsory for all between the ages of five and 13. The provisions of the Act were complied with in Hulland, more or less, but as in many rural schools until fairly recent years, where many pupils came from farming families, the three Rs took second place to the need for extra hands at harvest and hay-making.

Generations of Hulland children remember their teachers fondly, with affection and respect. Some of those teachers, and their charges are pictured below.

Above: Education was evidently a serious business then (c 1921). How grim they all look, especially those boys in the front row – have you ever seen such scowls! Mrs Evelyn Willetts, who kindly loaned this photograph and others, was then Evelyn Taylor, the diminutive figure at the centre of the group; at the time of writing a sprightly 94. Far right is the headmistress, Miss Hindmarsh. She will be having a word later with that lad in the back row who grinned at the camera.

Above: In 1923 the headmistress of Hulland school had no fewer than six pupil-teachers to assist her; though their supervision and training, combined with her own teaching and administration duties, must have made them a mixed blessing. Shown here are, rear row: Alice White, Evelyn Taylor, Bessie Allsop (of Atlow) and Mary Metcalfe; front: Agnes White, Alice's sister, and Evelyn Redfern, of Hognaston.

Life was spartan in the old schoolhouse, with a stove for heating and no piped water. An ex-pupil recalls older boys being sent to fetch water from the common well, pushing a rickety contraption made of a milk churn mounted on old pram wheels. This was a much fought-over chore, allowing a brief escape from lessons.

Junior school poses for the year photograph in 1950. They seem a chubby, well-nourished little group; their teacher, Alice Warner, is not long out of training college. Hulland Ward's own "Miss Read", she taught at the school for nearly 40 years and is remembered with affection by her pupils; "Always kind and helpful", as one such said. Miss Warner lives in retirement in View-dales Close. (Note the condition of the playground surface – scabby knees must have been endemic).

Back row, l to r: Colin Sellars, David Booth, John Bayliss, Tommy Walker, Alan Russell, Peter Robinson, Eric Massey. *Middle row, l to r:* Brian Thompson, Margaret Finney, Janet Hall, Pauline Sellars, Mabel Adams, Mabel Armishaw, Eileen Booth, Barbara Harrison, Roy Nash. *Front row, l to r:* Susan Booth, Doreen Fearn, ? , John Allsop, Robert Adams, Anne Walker, Janet Hough, Linda Fearn.

Opposite top: This school group is thought to date from the early 1920s. Unfortunately, no date is included on the sign-board, though there are more than the usual number of Eton collars in evidence. A further clue is that the young woman in spectacles (2nd left, back row) appears to be Miss Evelyn Redfern, one of the pupil-teachers in a previous photograph. Enquiries have failed to identify the pupils; perhaps someone recognises themself, a parent or grandparent?

Opposite bottom: The date of this group is known – 1949 – and the identity-of most members of it. *Front row, l to r:* Jean Hesbrook, Freda Fearn, Isobel Archer, Emma Wheeldon, Janet Gregory, Mabel Adams, Beverley Naylor. *Middle, l to r:* Margaret Allsop, Margaret Adams, Joy Archer, Gladys Booth, Joyce Sims, Joyce Finney, Margaret Hitchcock, Christine Wallace. Rear, l to r: ?, Adrian Robey; Robert Dale, ?, Roy Russell, Colin Wheeldon.

Above: On the occasion of the school's centenary, 20 March 1963, local dignitaries scrutinise the founding charter, with (l to r) Harry Harvey Dale, churchwarden; Mr Smithies, headmaster; Mr Heath-Smith, Director of Education; and the Vicar, Rev Post.

Below: On the same occasion, pupils show off their presentation centenary Bibles, with some looking more grateful than others.

Above: A scene of happy and orderly industry in Alice Warner's classroom at the old village school in 1947.

Right: An argument over the football at playtime.

Below: Alice's retirement in 1986, after 40 years of educating Hulland's young. Flanking her on the right is Mr Alfred Sims of the well-known Hulland farming family who shared with Alice their first day at the school; he as pupil, she as teacher. Left is the youngest junior, Angela Copper.

Left: This charming, dimpled foursome models the new school uniforms in the playground in 1974. Where are they now?

School outing to London, 1984.

Right: Huddled out of the wind under the National Gallery portico, Nelson's Column behind and *Below:* posed on the steps of No.10 Downing Street, with the girl in front glancing nervously behind lest Mrs Thatcher fling open the door and cry, "Shoo"!

Moving day at the old school, abandoned after nearly 125 years. Classroom furniture is stacked forlornly in the playground, awaiting the council van. A poignant moment, made the more so because the furniture was deemed too shabby for the pristine new school on the estate, and was to be distributed among the council's less-favoured establishments.

Pre-school and already competing! Easter Bonnet Parade, 1978. Evidence here, if such were needed, of much devoted and imaginative work by proud Mums to produce such a colourful line-up. A "tough time" indeed for the judges; not, perhaps, fully appreciated by little Jenny Crossland who looks distinctly underwhelmed by her success. 1978, where are they all now!

The New School

How schooldays have changed! Glance back a few pages to the stiffly-posed school groups from the early decades of the century and the expressions on those young faces, ranging from apprehension to truculence, with no hint of a smile. Having said that, it was, of course, a rare and solemn occasion, the class photograph; not a moment for displaying youthful high spirits. Cameras were almost as rare as motor-cars then and you didn't have your picture taken every day. If the headmaster was not himself an amateur photographer, as many were, a professional was called in. And the solemnity of those formal little groups lined up in the playground reflected the atmosphere within; studying them one can almost smell the chalk dust and hear the treble litany of times-tables being recited.

What could be in greater contrast to the pictures which follow...

They begin with the prerequisite for a modern school system – a bright, up-to-date, well-maintained building with sports field adjacent: the new Hulland Ward primary school, completed in 1983. The school is very much at the centre of things, figuratively and in fact, on the estate. Until the new village hall opened it was the only public building in the village with a hall roomy enough to accommodate fetes, fairs and other meetings, as well as the school's own out-of-hours functions.

The biggest change from the early years must be all the school outings and excursions which the curriculum allows and which are pictured here; all educational, of course, but how much more enjoyable than dry and dusty classroom lessons that older generations endured...

School Sports Day

This is 1997, but it could be any year – or at least, any year with a bright and sunny June day to sanctify the occasion. Sheer enjoyment is manifest; where young faces are frowning it is with concentration and the will to win. No uniform or "gym kit"; dress-of-the-day is the childrens' own leisurewear, and very colourful it is. No doubt some competitors grew rather hot, but hot children nowadays, with all that lightweight, easy-wash clothing, aren't as niffy as their parents and grandparents in similar circumstances were. Go on, admit!

Above: Full-pelt in the wheelbarrow race. Presumably they were loaded with something – concrete for the boys perhaps and polystyrene for the girls, or is that sexist?

A graceful bowling follow-through frozen by the camera in an almost balletic pose.

That skilful lensperson at the bowling alley again, catching the "cheese" just as it leaves a pair of small, chubby hands for a, presumably, shortish trundle.

A mystery event involving rows of chairs, sprinting, sheets of toilet-paper, and muddy knees.

We can see what this is: it's hockey...or is it croquet?

At another happy outdoor event, the School Fete, an appreciative parent thanks the headmaster and helps him cool off. (This must be by that same talented photographer who catches the microsecond of greatest effect).

The balloons go up, each with its message, to be returned in due course from the Cocos Islands. Or Bradley.

Tired but happy after a fun-filled afternoon. Mums, and a couple of Dads, collect their progeny, some Lutching trophies of the day.

There has to be the exception which proves the rule of no formal line-ups in modern schooling. In this case it is the Hulland Ward C of E Primary's soccer team which is proud to do so, resplendent in its new strip in the autumn term, 2000. Back row, l to r: Matthew Harwood, Gavin Astbury, Sam Small, Matthew Fernandez, Aiden Darné, Matthew Allcock, Cameron Godfrey, Matthew Coxon. Front row, l to r: Martyn Allcock, Callum Woolley, Shaun Holmes, Peter Boulton-Lear, Andrew Hollick, William Hall, Danny Macdonald.

Above: An informal line-up, more of a bunch really. School group arrive at Hathersage Youth Hostel for a 3-day study tour, September 1994.

A visit to Peak Cavern. The group gives their guide their undivided attention; something rarely afforded by kids en masse, and one wonders what he was warning them of – trolls, perhaps?

After the deep, claustrophobic confines of the cavern, a gusty, invigorating tramp over Mam Tor, well muffled against the wind. Edith Hough, one of the mandatory accompanying adults, admires the view. There's always one, isn't there, who rushes impatiently ahead and has to be called to heel to await the main body.

Proof positive of location on this occasion. What a charming group they make; just look at their beguiling, winsome little faces! But why, oh why, do they have to turn into teenagers...

Negotiating a tricky descent – some footpath! The grown-ups lend a hand.

Above: What a relief to rest those hot, aching feet. Like soldiers on a route march, the moment a halt is called – take the weight off! (What are they gazing at, up in the trees?)

Right: It's not all out in the open air, enjoying yourself. This is an educational trip, and written work is required. Students scratch heads and compose in the hostel's dining hall-cum-classroom.

Below: Juniors on an outing to Hartington hunker down to watch the ducks on the village pond.

Another school trip but further afield this time, to the National Railway Museum at York. On the left, a boring old diesel; while below a smiling line-up of senior girls (and aren't they a credit to their village!) perch on the running board, if that is the correct term, of an immaculately shiny locomotive named Cheltenham. For steam buffs – though of course you will know this already – she is a Southern Railway "Schools" Class 4–4–0, built in 1930 and withdrawn from servive in December 1962. She is preserved here in her original livery with her original SR number, which in her later British Rail days was 30925. There – something for everybody!

Two key members of staff share an anniversary, both having clocked-up 25 years of service. Mrs Shirley Dale (left), the school secretary, and Mrs Jean Redfern, senior meals supervisor, pose with their commemorative cake.

Below: At a presentation held at the Horns pub in Ashbourne, Shirley and Jean flank headmaster Steve Jackson.

The Scouting movement has been strong over the years in Hulland Ward, a factor not always given credit for its benign influence on the young, of this village and elsewhere. The activities have always, since its inception, channeled youthful energies in beneficial directions and, particularly in recent times, provided many outlets for out-of-school pursuits and interests in a community where "nowt much happens", as one juvenile was heard to complain. As with all village initiatives, it is only the community spirit of adults willing to give up some of their precious leisure-time to become involved which makes it work. Let tribute be paid here...

Hulland Cubs in camp at Osmaston in the 1980s.

Above: With Akela Pauline Birkett and Balu Margaret Seed, (this print is in soft focus).

Right: With Akela Graham Lee in charge.

Above: Old and new: 1st Hulland Scouts stage a concert party to entertain village folk in February 1956. Record proceeds were raised in support of a worthy cause since forgotten. Above l to r: Michael Heal, Roy Russell, David Hough, Reg Easter (Scoutmaster), Mick Ford, John Smith, Frank Johnson (Scoutmaster), Jim Booth, Robert Dale, Adrian Robey. Nearly 50 years on and pillars of the community! Once a Scout always a Scout; how nostalgic those baggy khaki shorts, toggles and BP bush hats!

Left: 33 years later and still winners. Hulland Scouts, District Football League 1989 season, proudly displaying their winner's shields. Rear, l to r: Barry Dias, Tim Davis, Neil Russell, Graham Stanley. Front, l to r: ? (sorry, how quickly fame fades!), Philip Smith, Andrew Lee, ?.

Ashbourne Carnival 1981. This bloodthirsty Hottentot tribe (above) are Hulland Cubs, scantily costumed on their float; one hopes the weather was kind that day, especially for the roped captive on the right (lunch?) lacking even boot-polish for cover. A more decorous theme (below) allows Guides to be included in this pierrot clown line-up.

Hulland Scouts and Cubs are presented with proficiency badges by District Commissioner Polly Day in 1986. l to r: Gordon Dick; Robert Wilson; Polly Day; Paul Birkett; Andrew Wilson. These photographs taken from the *Ashbourne News Telegraph* also announces the setting up of a Beaver Colony (for pre–Cub/Brownie age group) in Hulland Ward – the first in the District.

Right: Hulland Brownies line up for the start of the "Fun Run", Ashbourne Carnival, 1987; and *below:* leaving St Oswald's Church, Ashbourne for the St George's Day Parade, 1988.

Above: The Guides and Venture Scouts set forth, banners furled, for the same parade, Ashbourne 1988.

Below: From the eldest to the youngest in the movement. Hulland Beavers, now an up–and–running colony led by their Ahmeek Mrs Rose Dias, travel to Liverpool Docks in 1989 to pay a visit, at her captain's invitation, to their namesake warship, the frigate HMS *Beaver*. Here they line-up for a photograph beside her gangway.

Above: The Beavers "on deck" with their naval hosts, clutching rolled-up certificates and other momentoes of their visit.

Left: Talking of certificates, Ahmeek Rose scored a first in the Beaver world when presented with her Assistant Commissioner certificate aboard an HM Ship by her CO, Lt Cdr Richards, RN.

As the century opened the commonest form of rural transport was still Shanks's Pony. True, bicycle ownership had become widespread by 1900, as the cost of a cycle then, new or at least secondhand, was within reach of all but the poorest; though cycling was mostly thought of as a recreational activity rather than a serious means of getting about in all weathers. Carriers plied their trade, as they had done for centuries, by horse and wagon; conveying packages, newspapers and livestock including the two-legged kind, between villages and the nearest market town. In the 1900s Hulland Ward was provided for in this matter by Edwin Webster of Hognaston, a general carrier who served villages between Ashbourne and Derby. In this he was following his ancestors' calling, which the Websters of Hognaston had followed since 1692! Edwin's only rival then was the railway, which was not much use to you without a station or goods depot in walking or carrying distance.

The internal combustion engine ended all that, though like most new-age innovations it took a little time to reach rural areas (the first private motor-car to be owned by a Hulland Ward resident was a 1929 bull-nosed Morris, though some years earlier an even more antediluvean machine was supplied to Colonel Moseley of Hulland Hall). Today, Hulland Ward has two busy garages to serve the village's motorists, a majority: Hulland Ward Garage, established in the immediate postwar period and expanded from an earlier cycle shop; and Hulland Motors, opened in 1958.

But it was back in 1921 that Edwin, seeing where the future lay, purchased his first motor vehicle, thus founding the family business that was to become the Hulland villager's much-loved if sometimes derided principal link with the wider world. Much later that same internal combustion engine, which made possible fast, reliable and comfortable rural transport, came close to spelling its nemesis as private car ownership expanded and people spurned the local bus.

A regular bus service, however diminished from the apogee of the rural bus as lifeline, is still any village's greatest asset, as those unlucky enough to lose it have learned to their cost. Perhaps increasing congestion on our roads and the difficulty and expense of town-centre parking will yet see a resurgence of country bus routes.

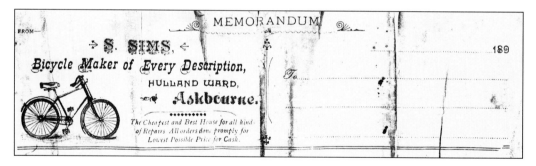

Foot of previous page: Samuel Sims, bicycle maker – letterhead 1890s. A true craftsman with the requisite skills to build a bicycle from scratch (or scrap!) to his customers requirements for an average cost of 25/–, (£1). Samuel supplied a machine to Bishop Smith (see Church chapter) for hard service in Equatorial Africa; not before diligently writing-off to the Palmer Tyre Co in London for advice on a suitable bicycle tyre for the tropics. Their reply is reproduced below, acknowledging the receipt of his undated favor".

THE PALMER TYRE LTD

CODE- 5TH EDITION A.B.C.
TELEPHONE No 788 HOLBORN.
TELEGRAMS, "INWHEELING, LONDON."

DEPOTS:
COVENTRY.
NOTTINGHAM.
BIRMINGHAM.
GLASGOW.

REGISTERED OFFICES,
121, 123, SHAFTESBURY AVENUE,
LONDON, W.C.

CYCLE TYRE DEPARTMENT,

103, ST JOHN STREET,
CLERKENWELL,

LONDON, E.C. ....June 10th........ 190-10

REF........JBD/EP........

Mr. S. Sims,
        Hulland Ward.
                Nr. Derby.

Dear Sir,

        We beg to acknowledge receipt of your undated favor, and in reply beg to state that in our opinion you could not do better than recommend a Palmer Special for use in West Africa, we ourselves confidently recommend it as the most reliable tyre on the market, and we advise it for use in Tropical Climates.

        We enclose herewith a small section of the outer cover which will give you a good idea of it.

        We shall be glad if you will kindly address any order with which you may favor us to our Nottingham Depot, where it will receive prompt attention.

        Assuring you at all times of our careful attention to any of your esteemed requirements

                Yours faithfully,

Enc.   FOR THE MANAGERS OF THE PALMER TYRE LTD

                        City Depôt Manager.

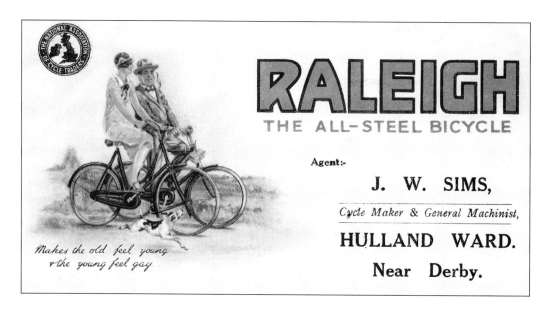

Above: A generation on, and son Jack is retailing a proprietory make, though he still describes himself as "cycle-maker". Note the slogan: "Makes the old feel young and the young feel gay". ("Gay" as in happy and light-hearted, of course). *Below:* A young Sims' customer poses proudly with his spanking new Raleigh at the foot of The Hollow; smartly suited, with gleaming boots and Eton collar, this is no village hobbledehoy; son of the manse, maybe?

The shape, sound and stink of things to come. This 1921 motor-cycle pioneer poses for the camera in an otherwise deserted Ward Gate. At left foreground is Anthony Dale's saddlery, and further up a horse is tethered – securely, one hopes – outside, aptly, the Nag's Head.

The times they are a-changing. Tradition encounters newfangled, and is not impressed. Horseman and motorcyclist (clad in early version of "leathers" and one o' they caps with a peak at the back, like,) exchange words at "Bottom End".

Left: Behind the wheel of this 1929 bull-nose Morris tourer sits proud owner Frank Dale (brother of Harry Harvey), the first private motorist resident in Hulland Ward.

Below: Hulland Ward Garage in 1948; then, and for some years to come, Hulland Ward's only garage and motor repair shop. As the present-day garage and service station boasts, it is one of the three oldest garages in the country, according to research carried out by ShellMex BP, and has been in the same family, save for a short period when a haulier had it, since the 1890s. The business was founded by Samuel Sims, a clock and bicycle-maker (see page 132). It was taken over by his son J W (Jack) Sims who sold and repaired bicycles. It was said of old Samuel that he would build you a spanking new bike from the rusted remains of three old ones!

The concern was bought from Harry Wheeldon, the haulier, after the war by the Russell brothers; the late Alan senior and Ron, Jack Sims' step-son, who extended and modernised it. Ron now keeps a proprietory eye on things from his nearby residence while his nephew, "young Alan", manages the day-to-day business.

Above: Hulland Ward Garage today.

Below: Until the late 1950s, parishes were responsible for road maintenance, with local roadmen allocated a "length" to maintain in good repair, like railway gangers. Here the Hulland Ward team pose in front of the old barn, now a private house, on the north side of the main road near "Top End", with their maintenance "rig" of tractor and trailer, about 1956. The man in the foreground digging his own private hole under the critical eye of the professionals is Mr Woodyatt, and that is his daughter posing in her smart but easily-soiled new outfit perilously close to the tarry trailer and its equally tarry attendants. Hulland's two roadmen, on the right, are Les Sims and George Watson.

Above: Hulland Ward's other garage, Hulland Motors, opened in 1954, with the forecourt and petrol pumps installed a little later. The extensive garage workshops are located behind this frontage, giving on to a spacious but rough-surfaced car and coach park, currently utilised by a local bus fleet. The newsagent, general store and mini-mart opened in 1986.

Below: Until recently a saddlery was established on the upper floor of Hulland Motors, continuing an old Hulland Ward trade and reflecting the popularity of recreational horse-riding in this, as in most, rural areas.

Generations of the Webster family of Hognaston have plied their carrier and, later, bus service between Ashbourne and Derby, serving the villages between. Theirs was always a small, local company, one of many such which operated, more or less successfully, between the wars. Sometimes ad hoc trading of routes took place between rival concerns, to mutual benefit and it was a succession of these together with the takeover of some abandoned routes which led to Webster's, by the outbreak of war in 1939, running services to Wirksworth and Derby via Hulland and Carsington; via Brassington to Ashbourne; to Matlock and Bakewell. Edwin Webster kept his small fleet running throughout the war; villagers still needed to get to shops, children to school and farmers to market. Fuel supplies were guaranteed for essential services and Websters picked up government contracts, one of which involved collecting Italian prisoners of war from their camp at Osmaston Manor (near Ashbourne) every morning and distributing them round local farms for agricultural labour. Evening trips to the cinemas to be found in every small town in those days were just as essential in maintaining morale among the war-weary.

Country bus services continued to prosper in the immediate post-war years, and Webster's was no exception. The family re-equipped their fleet with modern, comfortable 29-seater buses, opened a purpose-built garage and maintenance workshop at Hognaston Bridge, and Websters soon became the principal operator in the area. The 1950s were the heyday of small family-owned bus companies; increasingly thereafter the downturn set in, here as elsewhere, with increased car ownership the main cause. So the cycle of decline began: fewer passengers leading to less frequent services and routes being cut; fewer buses forcing more people to resort to their cars; and so on.

Edwin Webster died in 1963 at the ripe age of 92 – however many miles of highway must he have covered in his long working life! Some years before his death the business had passed down to Edwin junior and Harold, with Edwin's son Roy and Harold's daughter Caroline also later involved in the firm, the latter becoming the first female PSV licence-holder in the locality.

The company was taken over in 1973, but with the good name of Webster, built up over three generations, and as local carriers for many before that, being retained.

Down The Hollow, Webster's delivery van crunches over the gravel to Ashbourne.

Above: Edwin Webster Snr. poses, nonchalance failing to conceal pride, with his recently-acquired Garner busvan in front of Ashbourne's Green Man garage in 1922. The Garner was advertised as "The only vehicle built to carry passengers or goods without adding or removing equipment". So it appears to have been an intermediate stage in the evolution of carrier's cart to thorough-going passenger vehicle. It cost £855 – as much as two modest family houses at that date!

Below: This next Webster acquisition also had plenty of parcel space. It is a Bedford WHB of 1935. It was known affectionately to the villagers privileged to ride in it as "the henpen" (ladies clucking?) or "the boneshaker" (self-explanatory!).

Above: One of the three Duple-bodied Bedford saloons which formed the nucleus of Webster's modern postwar fleet which helped to maintain the firm's predominance on local routes. How evocative of those early postwar years are these trim, shapely little buses, winding through narrow country roads. How welcoming to the cold, wet traveller waiting at the stop as one hove into view, and as he climbed into its warm, stuffy interior, redolent of petrol fumes, damp clothes and a whiff of fragrant pipe smoke, to sink gratefully into a plushily upholstered, roomy and comfortable seat... that was travel!

Below: Webster's bus garage at Orchard View, Hognaston in the 1960s.

Chapter 7 – Carsington Water: A Landscape Reshaped

In terms of the historical scope of this story, the construction of Carsington Water on the village's doorstep is recent indeed, but its impact on the locality justifies inclusion here. A brief history of the reservoir's development and construction (including a major setback) follows, with apologies to older residents who are already familiar with it.

A glance at any Ordnance Survey map will reveal that Derbyshire has more than its share of surface reservoirs; the result of geography, landscape and an ever-growing demand for water for homes and factories to sustain modern living. So when proposals first emerged for what was to become Carsington Water few were greatly surprised, though there was some local opposition, notably from the Henmore Valley Preservation Society in alliance with the Country Landowners' Association and Derbyshire NFU. Also, serious discussions got under way in the mid-1970s, a time of dry summers and drought, and local folk in adjacent villages, particularly in Hognaston, were fearful of large tracts of smelly mudflats being exposed in warm, dry weather.

Above: A vanished landscape - view across Scow Brook Valley in 1980, just before the heavy plant moved in.

One could say that that prospect, at least, had receded by 1992 when the reservoir was opened.

A new reservoir in the locality was first mooted as far back as 1968, when the Water Resources Board concluded that: "...to avoid shortages in the late 1970s, the potential yields of Dove and Derwent would have to be developed by means of a regulating reservoir". Which is precisely what Carsington Water is: it takes water from the River Derwent in times of plenty; stores it and returns to the river when needed by means of a $6^{1}/_{2}$ mile subterranean pipeline connecting Carsington pumping station to Ambergate.

Before the existing site was settled upon, two alternatives were considered. These were at Brund, Staffordshire, on the River Manifold and at Ford on the River Hamps which, like the Henmore are also a tributaries. Though Brund would have been a cheaper option than Carsington, a deciding factor was probably that the former was located inside the Peak National Park, while Carsington is, of course, just outside. Also, flooding of the Scow Brook Valley (the true name: "Carsington Water" being a Severn Trent whimsy) would involve the inundation of only two farms – though many more were less drastically affected.

Once the public enquiries had deliberated and the go-ahead was given, work began in 1980 and ended abruptly in 1984 following a slippage of the dam embankment, which was too narrow-based and had been built on a bed of yellow clay. Very fortunately for Hognaston, overlooked by the embankment, the reservoir was barely half-full at the time. There followed a long hiatus while blame was apportioned, legal dispositions made and a new contractor hired. Work was resumed in 1989 and proceeded apace; dam construction was completed in September 1991 and the reservoir flooded. Meantime, building of an imposing Visitor and Educational Centre proceeded to completion in March 1992. Throughout the scheme, Severn Trent had been laying out amenities around the site; landscaping, siting nature reserves and planting half a million young trees and shrubs. These have now matured to a rounded, sylvan landscape enclosing a vast, contoured artificial lake, like a nobleman's Capability Brown-designed park writ large, except for the dinghies and sail boards tacking about on a bright, breezy day, and few would deny that it is good to look upon.

Carsington draws some 3-400,000 visitors a year, which obviously has implications for a stretch of otherwise quiet countryside, but it has to be said that the impact has been minimal so far: a little more traffic in the lanes at summer and weekends; a few new caravan sites and holiday flats scattered about. All the year round, local walkers, birdwatchers and people who just enjoy a little outing to feed the ducks, have this considerable amenity right on the doorstep, free of charge.

Well, actually, it cost £107 million, but you don't notice when it's included in your water rates, do you?

Right: May 1981 and construction gets under way as a jumbo crane appears on the skyline.

Above: Girdled in scaffolding, the draw-off tower creeps upwards.

Left: From the moment the site was acquired, Severn Trent began landscaping and planting the first of 500,000 trees and shrubs.

Above: Another Carsington amenity and a notable feature in the reservoir landscape is the henge erected by Severn Trent on "Stone Island", which is not actually an island but a promontory, accessible on foot. Designed by the architect Lewis Knight, the stones were erected in April 1992. They were carved from Derbyshire gritstone by craftsmen in Birchover, and are pierced with viewing holes to focus the viewer's eye on details in the landscape. The stones vary in height from six to $12\frac{1}{2}$ feet, with the biggest weighing $7\frac{1}{2}$ tons.

Below: A stone is swung across to be positioned precisely for lowering onto its base.

Following page: Aerial view of the Carsington dam embankment taken just after the collapse in June 1984. An enquiry concluded the causes of the failure to be a too narrow base to the embankment, also its bed of yellow clay; increasing pressure on it as the reservoir filled causing it to slip, fortunately when the water level was still low. Construction work stopped and was not resumed until 1988, using a new design for the dam.

Local people living near it needed some reassurance that the new construction would be safe. Severn Trent issued a pamphlet, with diagrams, explaining how the original embankment had failed and what changes were incorporated in the new design: crucially, digging through the yellow clay to a firm foundation and considerably broadening the dam base. Seems to be working so far.

Left: Even in these modern times it seems few major public works, from the Thames Barrier to the Channel Tunnel, are accomplished without exacting a toll in human lives. This monument placed near the Millfields visitor area commemorates the deaths of four young men who lost their lives during construction of the aqueduct.

Below: The draw-off tower, all 71 feet of it, is completed: May, 1990.

Above: Laying the base of the new dam embankment. Hundreds of tons of yellow clay, the unstable foundation which caused the original dam to fail, had first to be excavated.

Left: A whimsical view of work in progress, shot through the vent-hole at the foot of the tower.

Above: The decoratively paved circular viewing area located at the southern tip of the reservoir, close by the Millfields visitor area. The mounted stone at the centre commemorates the official opening performed by HM the Queen on 22 May 1992. (That is the control room at the top of the tower which a trick of perspective and an amateur photographer has perched atop the far wall).

Left: On 19 September 1991, in the shadow of the tower, a time capsule is buried by Patrick McLoughlin MP with Mr John Bellak, Severn Trent Chairman, looking on. The capsule's contents included contemporary newspaper cuttings, some children's drawings and – you won't believe this – a pair of Janet Reger knickers. What will the Martians or whoever's running the show in 2500 AD – make of those, one wonders?

Right: As local schoolchildren look on, the draw-off tower is in reverse mode when the first flooding began on 1st October 1991. In a powerful frothing torrent, the River Derwent comes rushing in.

Below: The water level inches up the tower. The reservoir took a day and a half to reach its capacity approaching 8,000 million gallons.

This page and following
Right: The official
opening of Carsington
Water Reservoir by HM
the Queen on May 22nd
1992. Her Majesty is
greeted and conducted
round the Visitor Centre
by Mr John Bellak,
Chairman of Severn
Trent Water.

Below: Queen Elizabeth
II and Mr John Bellak
inspect 'The Kugel', a
sphere of Bavarian
Granite completely
supported by water,
revolving in a socket.
The name Kugel comes
from the German for
ball.

Above: Her Majesty meets local schoolchildren...

Below: ... who are treated to a blow-out by Severn Trent to mark a memorable occasion.

Above: Nothing like Royalty for drawing the crowds! Visitors press eagerly, cameras aloft, for a glimpse of the Queen.

Below: The surfaced foot and bridle-paths which encircle the reservoir are good for year-round healthy walks, as these mid-winter trudgers attest; you can see how much they are enjoying it.

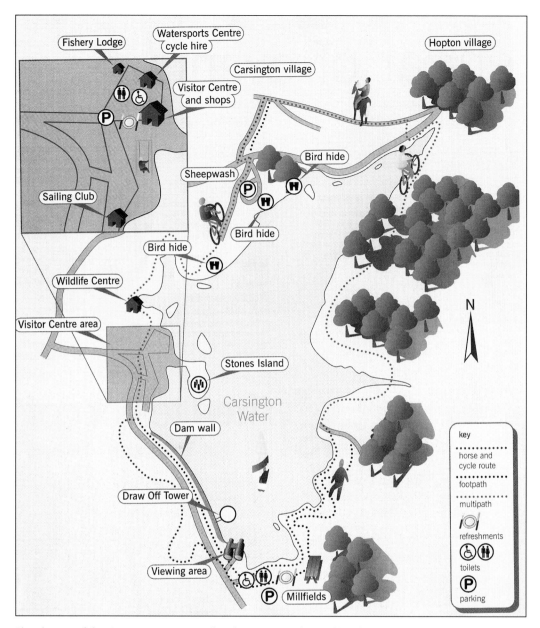

Sketch-map of the Carsington Water walk/ride route, 8 miles in all, affording open views and woodland paths, with picnic areas along the way. The route is well-marked; in fact one benefit, due either to munificence on the part of Severn Trent or, less likely, the district council, is that previously anonymous lanes adjoining it have been identified and labelled with smart new signs. Perhaps the names were dredged from locals' folk-memory; or perhaps where none could be traced a name was invented. Either way, they have a certain aptness: Broom Lane and Gorsey Lane could celebrate the contiguous botany; Benthead Lane is a bit steep in parts, so you might trudge up it with that comportment and Blind Lane, sure enough, peters out.

Some 40 years ago a local newspaper printed a feature titled *Mysteries of Derbyshire* in which reference was made to an isolated barn in a field between Kirk Ireton and Bradbourne. "Part stone and part brick", the writer says, "the barn has an ornamental roof and carved mullion windows giving it an ecclesiastic appearance..." and goes on to speculate about a possible connection with a Priory and monks in the neighbourhood. At the time of writing, the "barn" was in use as a cattle shelter and hay-loft.

It is now known that the curious little building was a 17th-century Dissenting chapel, which owed its isolated location to the hostility of the Established Church which banned dissenting congregations from holding worship within a decreed distance from parish churches. The chapel was on the upper floor, reached by a flight of stone steps; the ground floor being a stable to accommodate the mounts of the faithful who travelled far.

During the reservoir construction this rare and venerable little building narrowly escaped some over-enthusiastic bulldozing, but survived to be rebuilt a little distance from its original site, close to the Visitor Centre. Having had its roof heightened slightly and a small extension added at the rear, the Old Chapel is now in use as a Rangers Station. Many visitors are intrigued by it, with its carefully preserved and restored architectural features in marked constrast to the modern, sleek outline of the main centre buildings.

So concludes an "incomer"'s version of Hulland Ward and district's history of the previous one hundred years. It ends in the hope that it is recognisable as such to the many Hulland-born-and-bred among the villagers, and that they will be forgiving of the inevitable errors and oversights. Its object has been achieved if any one of them, perusing these pages, says: "Well – I never knew that!" It is the hope of both author and publisher that this book might stimulate interest in their neighbourhood of Hulland Ward residents who tend, like most of us, to take our home-ground for granted.

In the Introduction, the point is made that a little "digging" will usually reveal some rich seams of folk-lore, and that has certainly proved the case here. Some eight months of occasionally frustrating and mostly hugely enjoyable research has uncovered numerous arcane facts and stories – all, I hope, true – about the village and its inhabitants. One or two of them it was considered imprudent to repeat in print, but it's all in my notebook...

Perhaps, a hundred years from now, some hardy soul will undertake a record of Hulland in the 21st century. In the opening sentence of the opening chapter of this book it is remarked how relatively little change there was in the 20th, and how gradually that change occurred. Will that still be true of the present century? It seems unlikely. But who knows... it is safe to make predictions; we shan't be here, after all, in 2099. Or shall we, some of us, as medical science finds a cure for everything? Maybe then, as now, there will still be room in the church-yard...

LANDMARK COLLECTOR'S LIBRARY

Mining Histories

- Collieries of South Wales: Vol 1   *ISBN: 1 84306 015 9, £22.50*
- Collieries of South Wales: Vol 2   *ISBN: 1 84306 017 5, £19.95*
- Collieries of Somerset & Bristol   *ISBN: 1 84306 029 9, £14.95*
- Copper & Lead Mines around the Manifold Valley, North Staffordshire   *ISBN: 1 901522 77 6, £19.95*
- Images of Cornish Tin   *ISBN: 1 84306 020 5, £29.95*
- Lathkill Dale, Derbyshire, its Mines and Miners   *ISBN: 1 901522 80 6, £8.00*
- Rocks & Scenery the Peak District   *ISBN: 1 84306 026 4, paperback, £7.95*
- Swaledale, its Mines & Smelt Mills   *ISBN: 1 84306 018 3, £19.95*

Industrial Histories

- Alldays and Onions   *ISBN: 1 84306 047 7, £24.95*
- The Life & Inventions of Richard Roberts, 1789 -1864   *ISBN: 1 84306 027 2, £29.95*
- The Textile Mill Engine   *ISBN: 1 901522 43 1, paperback, £22.50*
- Watt, James, His Life in Scotland, 1736-74   *ISBN 1 84306 045 0, £29.95*
- Wolseley, The Real, Adderley Park Works, 1901-1926   *ISBN 1 84306 052 3, £19.95*

Roads & Transportation

- Packmen, Carriers & Packhorse Roads   *ISBN: 1 84306 016 7, £19.95*
- Roads & Trackways of Wales   *ISBN: 1 84306 019 1, £22.50*
- Welsh Cattle Drovers   *ISBN: 1 84306 021 3, £22.50*
- Peakland Roads & Trackways   *ISBN: 1 901522 91 1, £19.95*

Regional/Local Histories

- Colwyn Bay, Its History across the Years   *ISBN: 1 84306 014 0, £24.95*
- Crosses of the Peak District   *ISBN 1 84306 044 2, £14.95*
- Derbyshire Country Houses: Vol 1   *ISBN: 1 84306 007 8, £19.95*
- Derbyshire Country Houses: Vol 2   *ISBN: 1 84306 041 8, £19.95*
- Historic Hallamshire   *ISBN: 1 84306 049 3, £19.95*
- Llandudno: Queen of Welsh Resorts   *ISBN 1 84306 048 5, £15.95*
- Llanrwst: the History of a Market Town   *ISBN 1 84306 070 1, £14.95*
- Lost Houses in and around Wrexham   *ISBN 1 84306 057 4, £16.95*
- Lost Houses of Derbyshire   *ISBN: 1 84306 064 7, £19.95, October 02*
- Shipwrecks of North Wales   *ISBN: 1 84306 005 1, £19.95*
- Shrovetide Football and the Ashbourne Game   *ISBN: 1 84306 063 9, £19.95*
- Well Dressing   *ISBN: 1 84306 042 6, Full colour, £19.95*

Full details upon request. All orders are Post Free.

LANDMARK
Publishing Ltd ● ● ●

Ashbourne Hall, Cokayne Ave, Ashbourne, Derbyshire, DE6 1EJ England
Tel 01335 347349 Fax 01335 347303
e-mail landmark@clara.net web site: www.landmarkpublishing.co.uk

LANDM▲RK COLLECTOR'S LIBRARY

THE SPIRIT OF
ASHBOURNE:2

THE 20TH CENTURY IN PHOTOGRAPHS

Lindsey Porter

The Spirit of Ashbourne: 2
The 20th Century in Photographs
Lindsey Porter

Topics covered include: "Gone Shopping" – a look at the town's shops in days gone by; do you remember Woolworths, Carters Café, Dewhursts (opposite Wigleys Shoe Shop), Howell & Marsden, Smith's Wine House, Rushtons Furnishings? These and many more are featured; "Yards and Alleys" – scenes of the many houses which could be found in the town's yards, such as Malbons Yard, Stag and Pheasant Yard, Salt Alley and Tiger Yard; At work – more scenes of people at work in the town; Scenes of pubs; schools; sports; the nearby villages of Mayfield, Osmaston and Clifton are also included. A section on social highlights features a variety of events, dinners, fundraising and a host of similar functions.

Specifications: 192pp, Approximately 330 photographs, 246 x 174mm, hardback with wipe clean dustjacket.

Price £19.95

Published October 02